THE PATHWAY

TO BELIEVING

Books by

W. NORMAN PITTENGER

Approach to Christianity (*American edition entitled* The Christian Way in the Modern World)
Christ and Christian Faith
Christian Faith and Worship
Stewards of the Mysteries of Christ
His Body the Church
The Divine Action
A Living Faith for Living Men
Sacraments, Signs and Symbols
The Historic Faith and a Changing World
The Christian Sacrifice
Christ in the Haunted Wood
The Christian View of Sexual Behavior
Christian Affirmations
Theology and Reality
Tomorrow's Faith Today
Rethinking the Christian Message
The Church the Ministry and Reunion
The Episcopalian Way of Life
The Word Incarnate

BOOKS WRITTEN IN COLLABORATION

The Life of the Lord Jesus (with B. I. Bell)
The College Militant (with T. S. K. Scott-Craig)
The Faith of the Church (with James A. Pike)
What Is the Priesthood? (with J. V. Butler, Jr.)

The
PATHWAY
to
BELIEVING

BY

W. NORMAN PITTENGER, S.T.D.

THE **BOBBS-MERRILL** COMPANY, INC.
A SUBSIDIARY OF HOWARD W. SAMS & CO., INC.
Publishers · INDIANAPOLIS · NEW YORK

Much of the material found in these chapters is based on lectures given at a preparatory school conference in New England several years ago and later published as articles in *The Witness* during the year 1958. Other material has been used, in part, in a pamphlet published by The Forward Movement under the title *Jesus Christ God's Son Our Lord* (1951). The author and the publishers are indebted to the editors of *The Witness* and The Forward Movement for this use.

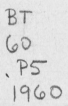

For

BRIAN AND GOODITH HEENEY

with love

PREFACE

IN THIS BOOK I HAVE TRIED TO SAY, IN PLAIN language, what it means to profess the Christian faith and how a modern man or woman can find his way to holding it. This is not a statement on behalf of any one Christian denomination; it is a statement of the basic affirmations upon which the great majority of Christian churches are agreed.

Most of the books which are available these days treat this matter in terms which the ordinary person has difficulty in understanding. In our time there is not that diffused knowledge of Christian ideas which half a century ago could be assumed by any writer on behalf of the Christian faith. So I have avoided technical language almost entirely; in the few places where some traditional phrase simply must be used, I have carefully explained its meaning.

The writer of these pages has taught for more than a quarter-century in a theological seminary. But besides that, he has been speaking to many groups of lay people, especially in schools and in colleges or universities. To do the latter is an education in itself, for one learns very soon that simplicity of presentation, use of contemporary illustrations and analogies, and awareness of the way people think and talk about life and its problems, are necessary if one is to establish any kind of contact with one's audience. In so far as this book does make that contact, it is thanks to the thousands of patient and friendly people who have heard its author speak and who have taught him how necessary it is to enter sympathetically into their ways of thinking and talking.

W. Norman Pittenger

CONTENTS

THE PATHWAY
TO BELIEVING

~ I ~

WHY SHOULD WE BOTHER
ABOUT RELIGION?

BACK in the middle of the last century, Henry David Thoreau went to live in a hut by Walden Pond in Massachusetts. While living alone in his hut he wrote a book that many of us were obliged to read when we were in school; it is called *Walden, or Life in the Woods*, published in 1854.

In recent years there has been a great revival of interest in Thoreau, for he seemed to have learned during his solitary days by Walden Pond something of what it means to be a real man. Thoreau was a remarkable person. He had little use for book-learning and he paid almost no attention to what people thought to be educated had to say about things. He believed that a man who lives by himself for a while, who looks at nature and thinks deeply about the meaning of *human* nature, can discover almost everything that there is to know. Most of Thoreau's friends, even Ralph Waldo Emerson, felt that he was a strange person. They were probably right. But as Emerson used to remark, Thoreau said some profound things and was himself a very "deep" man— he seemed able to get inside the feelings of the average person so that he knew from inside what it feels like to be a human being.

One thing that Thoreau said in *Walden* provides a good beginning for our own attempt in these pages to work our way through to a faith we can live by. What he said was that "most men live a

13

life of quiet desperation," a saying well worth our pondering.

"A life of quiet desperation . . ." However it may have been in Thoreau's day, there can certainly be no question that now, in our own time, a large number of people would agree that something important is being said in that phrase. Yet it does sound outlandish and exaggerated. But perhaps it comes pretty close to hitting the mark.

Most of us get along fairly well most of the time. We have our jobs, our homes, our families, our friends; we have lots of other things which keep our minds occupied and our hands busy. If anybody asked us how we are, we should probably answer quickly, "All right!" But is that really the case? For most of us there come moments, sometimes when we least expect them to come, when we have exactly the feeling Thoreau described in those words, "quiet desperation."

It is not very likely that we shall go out on the street and shout about it. We are not going to turn a Saturday night session with the neighbors into a "bull-session" about how we feel. We are hardly the sort of people who in the course of an afternoon call inform our hosts that we have that feeling. We do not like to talk about it at all. We keep quiet about it. It is nobody's business how we feel, anyway. But deep down, underneath all the surface life which we live, there is that strange awareness. Even when we act as if "we couldn't care less," as our English cousins phrase it, we know that something is the matter. Probably we just do not try to work it out. Life is a confusing and puzzling business, after all, and we must earn our wages, do our job, keep up the appearances, act like normal people. Still, some of the time, in the moments when the confusion and puzzlement press upon us, we *do* care. And then we have that sense of "quiet desperation" from which we simply cannot escape, try as hard as we can to find some remedy for our gnawing uncertainty and bewilderment.

All sorts of things contribute to this sense of "quiet desperation." Something goes wrong in the office or shop or in the plant or at school. We just do not know what to do about it. At home there are problems we must face: we can say that our husband or our wife or the children are fussy or tired, or perhaps we think that we ourselves are that way. The bills pile up and we do not see how we are going to pay them. The installment comes due on something we bought, and we are worried about how we can send the check that has to be sent. Our next-door neighbor is not so friendly as we had hoped he would be; he gets on our nerves, and his children are simply impossible. Something is said on a newscast or we see something in a television show which makes us wonder if the whole world is crazy; perhaps, from what we hear or see, it is going to blow up the day after tomorrow. We listen to a news reporter on the radio, or we read a commentator in the newspaper, and we get the feeling that everything is going to hell around us.

There are hundreds and thousands of things, and hundreds and thousands of ways, through which this feeling of disquietude comes upon us. I should be willing to bet there is not a reader of these pages who has not had just this feeling—and had it many, many times.

Of course, we ought not to exaggerate. Nobody feels this way all the time. And most of us, as I have already said, get along fairly well a good deal of the day or week or month or year. But the moments come. And when they come, we would give a lot to have some help. For the moments are thoroughly uncomfortable. More than that, we are likely to have a sneaking suspicion that in those moments we are much closer to the real facts, to reality itself, than in the times when everything seems to be "all right."

But what sort of help? Now I do not think that what we are looking for is a complete answer to all the questions, a complete solution to all the problems. Only a fool would expect that he could ever have all the answers and all the solutions. We know perfectly well that being men we are not likely to get them; and even if we did, we should not be able to understand them. We are humble enough to grasp that truth. Furthermore, most of us recognize that there are many questions which simply do not have answers, except the kind of answers that life itself works out for us. Experience is our only teacher in many areas of human life.

There is an old Latin saying, *solvitur ambulando*. It means that some things get solved just by our going along with them. And a considerable number of our questions can be solved only in that way. We live with the question for a while, perhaps for a good long while; and then we find that somehow or other it has answered itself. There are plenty of problems, too, which anybody with common sense knows cannot be answered completely and fully; so we just accept the facts as they are and go on living.

The help that we want in those moments of "quiet desperation" can be summed up in three simple words. What we want is some way to get and to keep a sense of *proportion* about life. What we want is to have a point of view—shall we call it a *perspective?*—which will make it possible for us to see things, including ourselves, not just in proportion to their real significance, but to see them from the right angle, to see them in the right way. What we want, above all, is some strengthening energy—some *power*—which will give us the stamina to stick it out when things get pretty bad; we want to be able to "take it," as we say, without feeling that the whole business of living is too much for us, without being obliged to acknowledge that life simply defeats us. There are the three simple words: *proportion, perspective, power*.

The need for proportion, perspective, and power is a silent witness to a very strange but very real truth about every one of us, and about all of us together. That truth is that man—every

16

man—and mankind—the whole race—are somehow or other incomplete. Something is lacking. We simply do not have, in and of ourselves, the capacity to develop a sense of proportion which will make us see things, and ourselves too, in terms of their real, not their imagined, importance. We simply do not have, in and of ourselves, the capacity to develop a point of view, a perspective, which will enable us to understand things, including ourselves, with honest and accurate vision, undistorted by our bad sight and our very individual preferences and prejudices. Above all, we simply are not able to generate, in and of ourselves, the power for brave and dignified human living.

Of course we can fool ourselves. A good deal of the time we do that anyway. It is fairly easy to slide along, taking it easy, claiming we never worry. Or it is possible to go whistling through life, boasting about our human dignity and proud that we are not in the clutch of circumstances. But is not that rather like the frightened little boy whistling as loudly as he can as he walks past the graveyard? Much of contemporary humanism, so called, resembles that little boy; it consists in loud whistling in the futile effort to keep our courage up at the very moment when we are scared almost to death.

Man is a pretty great figure in the world. There is no point or use in denying that patent fact. People who like to sneer at the human race are usually rather cheap people. Man can do, and he has done, a great deal; and he has done it against tremendous odds. We have a perfect right to be glad that we are men; and we have a perfect right to a kind of restrained pride in what man has been able to do during the long course of his history. Nobody should deny any of this.

But with all man's achievements, with all his grandeur, there is still something lacking. Pascal spoke of "the grandeur and the misery of man." Our grandeur is obvious; but, on the other hand, so is our misery. We *do* have that sense of "quiet despera-tion." So the truth remains true: man is incomplete. He *needs* something.

For one matter, man needs obvious things like food and friends. Everybody would agree to that. Without food, you would starve to death. Without friends, you would sink to a sub-human level. We are social animals, and our social-belong-ing is as much a part of our human nature as the fact that we are biological creatures. We could not get along without other peo-ple, in that we require their support and presence, but also in the sense that belonging with others provides us with an assur-ance of our humanity. The lone wolf is hardly a full man.

But we need other things not so obvious as food and friends. We need understanding and sympathy from others. We need love. All the psychologists these days are telling us this. Most emotional disorders come from a deep sense that we are not loved, that nobody cares, that we are "alone in the world," and that we should never be missed if we dropped out of existence. Everybody needs that understanding, sympathy and love; we can call it "acceptance." Even babies need it. There is a story—true or false, I do not know—of a hospital which employed an old and affectionate woman to take in her arms the babies in one of its wards, simply in order that they might not feel that they were not cared for and loved. It is not sentimentality, it is simply fact, that we are all that way.

Above all, we need to feel and know that in some fashion we belong in the world and that it is possible for us to live in it with at least a little dignity and decency. As a friend of mine once put it, men and women need some greatness to give a meaning to their littleness. It is this kind of awareness, deep down in the very root of our being, which can give us the strength to live through, and rise above, the day-by-day difficulties and prob-lems and questions which so constantly "get us down."

18

Now when I say that man needs God, I am talking what I conceive to be plain common sense. And the way to see that it is common sense is to begin by asking what we mean when we use that little Anglo-Saxon word "God" or its equivalents in other languages. It is not the word that matters; what is important is what the word stands for, the reality to which we point when we use the word.

As a simple fact, we can say that what people have meant when they use the word "God" is precisely a reality—or perhaps we should say, a Reality—that is big enough, strong enough, wise enough, good enough, to complete man's incompleteness. Of course a great deal more must be included in the meaning of the word "God," but for the moment I want only to stress the truth that people have concerned themselves with God because they have been convinced that there is a Reality who does just those things. Not that God has been thought of as man's slave, whose only reason for existence is to complete our incompleteness. A God of whom that could be thought would not be big enough, strong enough, wise enough, good enough, to do anything really important. It is otherwise; it is that the Reality with whom we have to do is the greatest, strongest, wisest, best of all beings; and *because God is that*, he does as a matter of fact complete our incompleteness.

If it is proportion we lack and that we know we ought to have and want to have, is it not true that proportion is really possible only for One who sees things as they really are, in their proper relations one to another?

If it is perspective we need, is it not true that perspective is possible only for One who does know the truth about things, the right and the wrong about them, the way they are related one to another in order of value and importance?

If it is power we are seeking, where can it be found except in One who is great enough to hold everything in control, strong enough to work through all things, wise enough to act in the right way in this and that spot, and good enough to bring about worthwhile results which will contribute to the welfare of everybody and everything? And *that* is what we mean when we say that it is only God who can explain and make sense of the whole business of life, give us the things that we really need, and thus fulfill and complete our incomplete human lives.

One of the interesting developments in the modern world is that more and more people are beginning to realize this. They may have rejected the childish religious ideals they were once taught; and very likely they are entirely right in doing so. They may never have been taught any religious ideas at all. They may never darken the doors of a church or a synagogue, although an increasing number of them are beginning to do just that. But however it may be, more and more people are concerned once again about the things in which religion has always been interested. They are looking for what we have called proportion and perspective and power; they want completion for their incomplete lives. They are beginning to wonder whether perhaps, after all, granted the distortions and perversions and difficulties religious faith may have had for them in the past, there is not something in it, after all.

Such people are coming to recognize that when it is a question of *big* things, concerning who we are and what we are and why we are here and what we can make of life, we simply cannot afford to be small-minded. We must try to get behind the things we reject or don't understand or don't like, to the reality which may be there. We are beginning to feel, with a strangely perplexed mind and heart, that the "old folks" of yesterday and the day before possessed something we have lost and which we very badly need to find again. Maybe it *is* God we really need.

We can all of us be greatly helped by a straightforward and

clear statement of the big and basic affirmations which the Christian Church has been making for two thousand years; and all of us can be aided in seeing ways in which those affirmations can be made to come alive for us in our own present-day experience.

Just as well as the next person, I know that a great deal of what the Christian Church has said in the past is, for us today, plainly and simply incredible. We get nowhere at all by attempting to deny that fact. There are reasons for it. After all, we have learned much about the world and how it came to be; we have also learned much about ourselves and about what makes us tick. There has been an enormous accumulation of new knowledge, especially during the last hundred years; and each of us must take account of it, if he is not going to be an ignoramus or a fool or a die-hard conservative who shuts his ears to anything he does not like. We cannot help being modern men and women who live in the middle of the twentieth century; and there is no reason why we should suppose that we ought to try to live with patterns of thought that served perfectly well a couple of hundred years ago, but that are entirely out of date in the nineteen-sixties.

Such a faith as we can live by today will not be very different, however, from what our Christian ancestors lived by. They often expressed it in other words from the ones we might feel appropriate; they mixed it up with a great many ideas and beliefs entirely natural in their time but unacceptable in ours. But the heart of the matter was pretty much the same as it is, or may be, for us today.

For there is one thing about religion that is perfectly plain to those who look at its history in the affairs of men. Religion is never devised or made up out of the whole cloth. It is handed on; it grows. New ways of thinking about things, new ways of putting things, new ways of believing things, emerge out of the old ways. Otherwise they are *ersatz*, fakes which simply cannot "deliver the goods."

This development, this handing-on, this growth, is what is meant when we talk of Christianity as a *tradition*. A tradition is something that is "handed on"; and as it is handed on, it develops and grows. Of course, it may be handed on in a dead, uninspired, and uninspiring manner. It may be looked at simply as archaeology. But I am not interested in that; and I am sure that my readers will not be interested, either. On the other hand, it may be handed on in a living, vital, and vitalizing manner. It may be seen as being in itself—this tradition—a living, dynamic, vital, and vitalizing thing; it may be seen as a growing and developing tradition. It is like a human body, or it ought to be. In one sense, the human body remains the same through the years of our life; it has certain persistent marks, certain identical and identifying characteristics. That is how we know what body it is, to whom it belongs, how it can be named. Yet it is also growing and changing, adapting itself to new situations and responding to new demands which these situations make upon it. That is how we know that it is a living body, not a dead or dying one.

⟡ 2 ⟡

WHAT IS RELIGION ABOUT?

WHAT man needs is a religion which is true and which, being true, can provide the consciously known and experienced Reality which will complete and fulfill our human nature.

Just to say "religion" is to say either too little or too much. There have been a great many religions in the history of the human race, and there are a great many of them in the world today. Some of them seem to have been good and some of them seem to have been bad. Some of them have been ways in which men have been enabled to develop and grow towards fulfillment, but some of them have had a negative and inhibiting effect on those who held them. Religion, as a word, is only a description of a certain kind of attitude and a certain way of thinking, which takes many different forms depending upon which religion we are talking about.

This is why there are few things quite so stupid as to urge that what is needed is "a religion"—any old religion. Today a great number of people can be found who talk in this silly fashion. One distinguished national leader, some years ago, said that if only everybody had some religious faith, he for his part did not care what that religious faith was. Now this was a very empty utterance; for it may very well be the case that certain religious faiths are devastating in their result.

Nazism made a religious impact on millions of people and its result was appalling. Similarly, there have been primitive religious cults which have been morally disastrous and humanly distorting. Nobody ought to want his friends to accept such a cult just because it can somehow be described as "a religion." What we want is not any old religion; what we want is a religion which in some fashion can be seen as *true*—a religion which corresponds with as much of the facts as can be, which secures the right and proper development of man, which indeed has at its core the completion and fulfillment of human nature and not its destruction or deterioration.

So we have two jobs to do. The first is to attempt a sketch of the characteristic marks which may be seen in the religious *thing*, whatever it is. For it is possible that all religions do tend to follow a certain pattern, however they may vary as good or bad religions.

In the last analysis there are three such marks or characteristics. Every religion which has claimed the allegiance of men— whether it has been for their good or for their hurt—has had some sort of *creed*, some sort of *cult*, some sort of *conduct* which it commends and expects. Each of these it has regarded as of the highest importance. Or we might use another letter—"d" this time—and say that every religion which men have followed has taught certain *doctrines*, has engaged in certain *devotions*, and has expected its adherents to follow certain *disciplines*.

Every religion which has ever captured the allegiance of people has had some beliefs or teachings, some affirmations or assertions, which have been taken to be highly important. "Creed" comes from the Latin word *credo*, which means "I believe"; "doctrine" comes from another Latin word, which means "teaching." All the religions which men have held believe or teach something. What they believe or teach naturally differs from religion to religion. They do not all say the same thing, but they do all say something. So we shall expect to find, when we read about a religion of any kind and in any place, that there will be beliefs or teachings which the people who adhere to that religion are expected to accept. When a soldier or sailor during World War II happened to land on some island in the Pacific and saw there a great many religious practices he had never run into before, one of the questions which naturally sprang to his lips was, "What do these people believe, anyway? What do their old men or their priests or their leaders teach them?"

In the second place, every religion has a cult or devotions. Here once more we are using words which are derived from the ancient Latin language. "Cult" comes to us from *cultus*, the word by which Latin-speaking peoples described gatherings of men and women to engage in what we should call "acts of worship"; a *cultus* was a social group engaging in religious practices which were thought to be necessary or useful or desirable. Again, "devotion" comes to us from Latin; its root-meaning is the dedication of somebody to the worship of whatever he regarded as divine. So "devotion" essentially comes to signify what we should call prayer. Let us remember that at the moment we are not concerned with what or whom people worship, or with how they picture the object of their worship, or with the particular techniques they may use in their prayer. The fact is that those who belong to a given religion worship and pray; they unite in social groups (primitive religion especially is more likely to be social in nature), or in private to "devote themselves" (and some of the higher eastern religions put greatest stress on this individual aspect), to the end that they may be related in one fashion or another to whatever it is they happen to regard as divine and hence as worthy of their worship and devotion. The fact of such rites, the engaging in worship, the saying of prayers, is one of the most obvious facts about religions all over the globe and—so far as we can trace human history—in all ages of men.

The third characteristic is conduct or disciplines. Every religion has something to say about these. And again the words are

25

from the Latin. The word "conduct" signifies a way of behaving or acting; "discipline" means a rule or plan or scheme or design which is to be followed and which therefore dictates and controls action or behavior. In each religion there are things which one does, manners or ways of acting, which are thought to be right and proper; they are, so to say, "pleasing to the gods" or they are "according to the will of God." Our soldier or sailor on his island in the Pacific saw this too. The natives had certain agreed kinds of behavior; they followed certain rules which were binding upon them. If he had asked about this behavior and the rules which governed it, he would have learned that they were supposed to be tied in with what the inhabitants believed about the gods they worshiped, about nature and about life, about who they themselves were and what they were expected to do, so that they might live as they ought.

It is not only religions, in the usual sense in which we employ the word, which are thus to be described. Every way of life or design for living which has secured the allegiance of men and women has followed the same general pattern.

In the days when the Nazis were in power in Germany, visitors to that land used to notice that the Nazi movement had things to teach, and members of the Party had to believe them. It also had great rallies and ceremonial meetings, in which the members participated regularly, securing from their participation a sense of belonging to and dedicating themselves in the service of their Fuehrer and the principles which he enunciated —and this really amounted to an act of worship and a personal devotion, even if the god worshiped was the false embodiment of the heathen god of blood and soil. And the Nazi movement had a rigid discipline, with rules of conduct which were austere and demanding; every party-member was expected to follow these without question.

The same pattern may be noted in the communist who regards

the communist way of life as the true one. I myself have known few Russians, but I have known some Americans and Canadians who were dedicated members of that "party"; and I used often to think that in one sense they were the most "religious" people I had ever met, even though I regarded their "religion" with horror and dismay. For they had a set of beliefs, a creed, to which they were absolutely dedicated; they were regular and unfailing in their participation in meetings of their "cell" and in the party rallies which acted as a great stimulus to their loyalty to their beliefs; they were utterly devoted to what they were convinced was the movement of history in the direction of the "classless society"; and their conduct was as rigidly controlled and as obedient to the standards they had been set as that of any religion in the history of the human race.

For man has a mind, and he has emotions, and he has a will. He thinks certain things, he feels in a certain way, and he decides he ought to do this or that. It is, of course, complete nonsense to attempt to cut men up into three sections and say one section of him does the thinking, another the feeling, and a third the willing. In philosophical and psychological jargon, that would commit the old fallacy of the "three faculties"; and no respectable philosopher or psychologist, no man with common sense, wants to talk in that fashion any more. But it is obviously true, all the same, that man in the wholeness of his personality does in fact think and feel and will. Perhaps we should put it this way: man as a whole is a thinking, feeling, and willing animal; it is the way in which all this has been developed, and the way in which all this is ordered and patterned in his nature, which distinguishes him from the apes.

Thus it is not only appropriate but inevitable that a man's religion, which has to do with his total personality because it claims his allegiance and secures his dedication of self, should follow the pattern we have described. Man is bound to respond through his mind—that is, through certain beliefs. He is bound to respond through his feelings—that is, through certain emotional reactions which are expressed and strengthened in cult and devotion. He is bound to respond through his will—that is, in his intentional and purposed acceptance of and his following through some disciplines or rules which govern his action and behavior.

Religion makes its appeal to the whole man. It makes its appeal to, and finds its expression in, each of the ways in which man himself lives and moves and has his being. A religion—any religion which has mattered in human history or in contemporary experience—has claimed the whole man and has involved the whole man in his religion, whatever it may be.

The religions which have been significant in the history of the human race have been those which do not emerge as entirely new creations by some one person. They are the religions which have had a "tradition"; that is, they have been handed down, even when in the process they have developed and grown and sometimes have changed almost beyond recognition. Even Christianity in its earliest stages was largely indebted to Judaism. Students of the subject have often called religions of this type "the positive religions." By this they have meant that such religions have not been devised by this or that great thinker or taught to people as if they had no rooting in past history; on the contrary, they have been the "founded" religions, established in the past and growing on into the future.

For some reason, the details of which we may perhaps leave to experts in the subject and especially to those who have made a profound study of human psychology and sociology, men do not seem to respond very favorably to religions which are presented as brand new. For one thing, they have felt that such a new religion did not speak to the depths in their personality; it was shiny, bright, glittering, but did not appear to be able completely to satisfy. Perhaps this response is silly; nevertheless, it seems to be the response which is very frequently found. Again, men have somehow wanted at all times in their long history, to be associated with movements that relate them to their racial past. However we may like it, the plain truth seems to be that the "old time religion" has a greater appeal to most people than something that is "new-fangled." Of course, this can lead to an unthinking conservatism which is nearly as dead as the dodo. On the other hand, it may speak to us of an awareness, deep down in our human life, that we do belong together—not only with our contemporaries but also with those who in the past have made us what we are.

At the same time, religions which have managed to continue their hold on men and women through successive ages have been open religions. By this term I mean that they have been religions which have not been entirely out of touch with contemporary life and contemporary problems and contemporary ways of seeing things.

Some of the great religions of the East, as well as some versions of Christianity today, are good illustrations of this. When a religion loses touch, it tends to become stereotyped and unattractive. It may retain its hold on some few die-hards, but the newer generation is not likely to find it appealing. Whether it keeps up to date by incorporating some of the new ideas in its own structure, or whether it does so by seeking continually new kinds of relation with people in their new situations, it must not let itself become simply dated, for that is the same as saying that it is *passé:* it has had its day, and that's that. The role of religion in human life has never been merely the consecration of the past for its own sake, any more than it has been the worship of the present for its sake; it has been a strange combination of the wisdom of the past and the vitality of the present.

All this is reflected in the place that is taken in the great religions by the two types of leader they have had. For convenience we can indicate these types by using words familiar to us in the Western world: "priest" and "prophet." The former, the priest, has been the man concerned above all with the continuities, the respect for the past, the maintenance of the great emphases which the tradition embodies. The latter, the prophet, has been the man who speaks the "new word" for the new time; he has had, for his principal interest, the relating of the tradition to the changing circumstances and the novel demands which those circumstances have brought forth.

Both of these seem to have been necessary. There has always been the man who kept the religion "going," with its given creed, cult, conduct; who was the repository for the wisdom of the past with its teaching, its devotion, and its disciplines. And there has always been the emergence, time and time again, of the man who could not rest content with things as they have been but who wished above all else to make the religion's teaching and worship and standards of behavior vital and compelling because they were related significantly to "new occasions" and "new duties." If for the moment we use specifically Christian language, we can say that the priest has been the man who represented and spoke for the heritage of our Christian past, while the prophet is usually not ordained but simply appears; "God This is why, again in Christian terms, the priest is ordained or set apart by the institutional Church to carry on its business, while the prophet has been the man who had "a new word from God." "God sends him" when and as God wills to send him.

More generally, the priest without the prophet would encounter the danger of simply running the machine; the prophet without the priest would run the danger of going off on a wild goose chase. If a religion has both of them, honors both of them, uses both of them, then it is likely to be deeply rooted in the past from which we have emerged, alert to the present in which we now live, and concerned also with the future to which we are inevitably moving. Such a religion is an impressive thing and speaks meaningfully to men and women, because every man and woman willy-nilly is a strange combination of past, present, and future and needs a religion which will enable him to live with that surprising but inescapable fact.

That is to say, one of the tests of a religion may very well be its capacity to keep these two elements in proper balance. But there are other ways in which we may apply tests to the many religions which have appeared in human history and still command the respect and devotion of their adherents.

⚘ 3 ⚘

AREN'T ALL RELIGIONS TRUE?

Nothing could be so silly as to assume that all religions, simply because they are religions, must necessarily be "a good thing." An old classical poet was perhaps nearer the fact when, contemplating what so much religion had done to men, he said that "great are the evils which religion brings with it." Barbarism, superstition, evil behavior—all of these have accompanied and resulted from religion.

Of course, if we have the wit and the wisdom to discern it, we can see that deep underneath these superficialities, far more abiding than the barbarism, superstition, and evil behavior, there is something about religion which is highly significant and profoundly true. For however distorted may be their way of stating it or expressing it, the religions of the world all bear witness to the presence in the affairs of nature and in the lives of men of something which is more real, more enduring, more important than men or their world. All religions testify to some dim awareness in men of every race and clime that there is a Reality upon whom human creatures do in fact "depend" for their very existence, and into relationship with whom they must somehow enter if they are to reach fulfillment and completion.

The appalling aspect of it all is that so often the religions which men have accepted have sought for that relationship by techniques which distort human life or deny its place and value in the scheme of things. The terrible fact is that many of these

33

religions have also equally distorted pictures of the nature of that Reality and hence have led their adherents to degrading practices and absurd beliefs. Thus it is perfectly right for us to maintain that some religions have been pretty bad, on the whole, while others have been pretty good, on the whole. But how are we to determine whether a given religion is good or bad? This is the second of the jobs mentioned in the last chapter.

I suggest this as a possible beginning to the answering of that question: the religions which make a man less of a real, "honest-to-God," man are the religions which are pretty bad; the religions which make a man more of a real, "honest-to-God" man are the religions which are pretty good. To be a real man— to be what I have even ventured to call an "honest-to-God" man— means that one is becoming more and more a rounded, developed, well-integrated, genuinely "healthy" sort of person. I do not want to suggest, or even seem to suggest, that by "healthy" I am talking about physical health in and of itself, although that is something we ought not to despise. The point is that a man who is truly "healthy" is a man who has that inner quality which comes precisely when he is approaching real proportion and real perspective and when he is possessed by a strength or power which enables him to face life, accept it, and make of it a thing of dignity and beauty.

But if this is to happen to anyone, he must be rightly adjusted, properly related, to the way things actually are in this world of ours. Or, in another way of saying the same thing, he must be so in rapport with the environment in which he lives that there is a healthy give-and-take between that environment and himself.

By the word "environment" I mean not only the things we see and taste and smell and touch and hear; I mean also the unseen things which are also really there: things like goodness, love, courage, beauty, truth, and their terrible opposites of which

34

we also are conscious, like evil, hatred, cowardice, ugliness, and falsehood. Above all, I mean by "environment" the Reality, whatever it may be, which is in and behind *all* these things and in which every one of us necessarily lives and moves and has his being.

If a man has the wrong sort of adjustment, an improper kind of relationship, to his environment, he will very likely be a sickly specimen of the human race. Maybe not right away or all at once, but sooner or later, the man who prefers falsehood to truth, or ugliness to beauty, or evil to good, is going to be somebody the human race is ashamed of. Why is this? It is because he has wrongly related himself to truth, which is a deeper reality than falsehood; he is adjusted improperly to the structure of things; he has mistaken something in his environment which is debilitating and damaging for something enriching and upbuilding. His easy-going, ready-to-hand adjustment to falsehood as if it were what it is not, his acceptance of it and his living in terms of it, will find him out in the end. *That* is the kind of man he will eventually become.

In other words, a religion that does not help a man in every way to become the finest person he is capable of being is a religion that is either false or seriously vitiated by error. On the other hand, a religion which helps a man to become a true, full, rounded, balanced, "healthy" human being, in association with his fellows, is a religion that has some claim to being true.

There are three things which we ought to be looking for in a religion, if we are concerned to find one that can validly make a claim upon our allegiance.

The first one has to do with *truth*. A religion that is worth our bothering about as being close to a true religion, is a religion that speaks the truth. It does not lie about life. It does not deny the facts. It is not afraid to let its adherents think as hard as they can about what it says, to test it, and, so far as possible, to prove it for themselves. A valid religion is a religion marked by the spirit of truth.

Now a religion like Hinduism, whose native home is India but whose influence is being felt in many other lands, even in the United States, says that the world of stuff—sticks and stones and material things that we bump into every day—is an illusion or a dream. It does not say that the world of stuff simply does not exist; but it does say that it belongs to the realm of *maya*—which means, we are told, a kind of "play" or "dream-world" which must be negated if we are to get to that which is really real.

One would not wish to accuse any individual Hindu of telling a falsehood; but one can say that a religion which talks in this fashion is falsifying the world that we actually know and experience, that we perceive and feel; that we cannot avoid and that we ought not to evade. Furthermore, the way in which the believer in Hinduism behaves when he is in contact with sticks and stones and material things—which, by and large, seems to be the way the rest of us behave—shows that for all practical purposes the stuff-world *is* there and cannot be got away from. So he is obliged to act a lie; for if his theory is true, his practice is false, while if his practice corresponds with the facts, his theory is untrue.

On the other hand, a religion like Judaism or Christianity accepts the fact of a material world. Such a religion insists that sticks and stones, the stuff-world, is real. It recognizes that we must reckon with that world whether we happen to like it or not. That is to say, Judaism and Christianity, in this respect at least, are truer than Hinduism. And there is no way in which Hinduism and the other two can be reconciled at this point, for they start from different assumptions and proceed to different conclusions—and "never the twain shall meet."

36

The second thing which a good religion ought to do is to allow men *freedom*. After all, whatever else may be said, every man feels that in some sense and to some degree he is a free agent. His freedom may be limited and restricted, not only by the circumstances in which he is placed, the heredity that is his, the education he has had, the family influences that have helped to mold him, and many other similar things; but also by his own previous decisions and actions—all of which have gone far to make him what he is.

Things of all sorts get in his way and frustrate him. Everybody knows that. But deep down inside, he feels that he is meant to be, and that to some degree he already is, a free man. He believes, and he lives as if he believes, that he is able to make choices, that he can say "yes" or "no," and that his saying one or the other of these has meaning because it reflects a real fact about him. Even when he is forced to do something he does not like, his spirit or his mind (as we often put it) can remain free. For

> Stone walls do not a prison make
> Nor iron bars a cage.

Define freedom in any way you wish, provided that you still leave to the word some real significance, and you must take into account the fact that people both want and feel themselves to be free agents in some important sense, despite all the restrictions, limitations, inhibitions, frustrations, with which they are met when they try to act on their choices.

Now a religion like Mohammedanism is open to grave question precisely at this point. That religion denies to man any genuine capacity for choice, because it views him as the determined instrument or tool of Allah—an instrument or tool which must accept *Kismet* or fate because there is nothing else to do. Christians have often seemed to speak in the same way, but the fact is that they have never really denied the basic freedom of man; even when they have spoken of man's highest freedom as found in his acceptance of the will of God. To say that God's "service" is "perfect freedom" is not to say that men are to be considered passive tools in God's hands. On the contrary, it is to say that when they themselves willingly and gladly surrender their wills to God, they find that they are released from faithless fears and worldly anxieties (as an old prayer puts it) and that they become truly free, for their choices are now in accord with the best that could be and they are on the way to becoming full and complete men.

The way in which popularly taught Mohammedanism puts it, however, is quite different from this. Freedom is really an illusion from which we ought to escape; we ought to be slaves of Allah, who is seen as a compassionate but in the long run essentially dictatorial deity. In Judaism and in Christianity, on the other hand, there is a strong insistence on man's capacity to respond with a "yes" or a "no"; and there is also a recognition that man is not only responsible for the kind of answer which he gives, but also that he is really making a contribution—good or bad as the case may be—to the accomplishment of God's purposes in the world. And a religion which talks that way is truer than a religion that fails to take due account of this patent awareness of freedom, with its corollaries in a sense of responsibility and answerability for the choices we make.

The third characteristic which we have a right to look for in a religion which makes a claim on our allegiance, is the spirit of *love*. By this I do not mean a sloppy sentimentalism which nauseates any self-respecting person when he sees it or is the object of its expression. I mean, on the contrary, a strong and positive concern for others, an active desire to advance their welfare, and a willingness to do all one can to help them be the best that they have it in them to be. That is what real love is all about. That is the kind of love we wish to have shown to us; that is the kind of love we feel we need if we are to be full and

38

complete men. Mere sentimentalism, mere feeling of vague generosity, mere gentleness without activity through which it is expressed, simply will not serve.

Now the trouble with a religion like Buddhism is that while it talks a good deal about "love," it means something weaker than the love about which I have just now been speaking. For its notion of love is founded on its view that desire is the root of man's troubles and that by killing desire we can be freed from these troubles and live with serenity in the midst of this world.

Buddhism advocates gentleness, but by this it seems to suggest a kind of unconcern; it speaks of sensitivity, not as an active business but as a passive awareness. In their history Buddhists have not shown an active, vigorous, out-going care for men and women. The religion has not led to any struggle for giving to the underprivileged and dispossessed the right they have to develop themselves toward a joyous, free, and decent existence. Even the attitude of non-resistance, which can be turned into a valuable positive weapon for the good, can result in indifference and acquiescence to situations and circumstances that would seem to demand positive action in the resistance of evil.

Nor do I think that this is simply the difference between the passive Easterner and the active Westerner. It is really integrally related to the religious faith which marks the Buddhist. It would be more accurate to say that Buddhism—and Hinduism, too, in so far as it approximates Buddhism in this kind of passive view of love—has made many Eastern peoples what they are. Now that the allegiance they once felt for this religion has been weakened, they are showing that they too can have a positive conception of caring and an active understanding of human relationships. Nehru, indeed, has often said the religious outlook in India has done more than anything else to leave millions in poverty and degradation.

Of course, there are many good things in both Buddhism and

Hinduism, as there are also in Mohammedanism. But the sad truth is that the basic assumptions of these religions tend to deny important facts; and that insofar as Buddhism stands for an essentially negative and passive attitude, it is likely to do more harm than good so far as countless thousands of people are concerned.

On the other hand, a religion like Christianity, which has at its very heart (however badly it may express it in action) the conviction that positive, out-going love is at the heart of reality, is a religion that has a claim upon us such as other religions cannot make. But further, a religion like Christianity which insists upon the "divine imperative," calling us all to show such outgoing, positive, active love in our relations with others, to love our neighbor as ourselves, is a religion which at least in principle is more likely to promote justice, good-will, happiness, and responsible activity among men and nations.

Now, some religions are better in practice than in theory, and some others are better in theory than in practice. At the moment, however, we are concerned with what the several religions actually do say; we are interested in the basic ideas, the underlying assumptions, which are at their heart. And these are of extraordinary importance—for "as a man thinketh in his heart, so is he." As a religion seriously interprets life and its meaning, so in the long run will that religion become in actual practice. Theory and practice, belief and behavior, conviction and conduct, are pretty closely related in human experience; and sooner or later the theory, the belief, the conviction, will determine the practice, the behavior, and the conduct. This is why the first set of three are in one sense more important than the last set of three, for the first set finally determines what the second set will be.

What a religion has to say about truth, freedom, and love—and the way in which its emphasis, such as it is, on these things is stated and expressed—will depend in the long run on whether that religion is built around the ideas of men or is built around facts of life and experience. So we can ask the question: does this or that religion reckon seriously with what has happened and is happening in the world?

Facts are of various sorts, of different kinds; but the facts about which I am now speaking are the hard, inescapable facts of human history—what a great thinker of our century, the Baron Friedrich von Hügel, once described as "historical happenedness." A vital religion is not only one which is unafraid of truth, which guarantees because it respects human freedom, and which lives and moves in a spirit of love; it is also likely to be one based upon historical events in the hard, crude, rude, harsh world which we all know so well and from which we can never escape. If the religion which shows concern for truth, respect for freedom, and recognition of the necessity of love, can point to, because it bases itself upon, a real human life in which these three things somehow or other got themselves embodied, that religion has a very high claim upon us.

Furthermore, a religion which does not thus point, because it does not base itself upon such a real human life, is a religion which is in a somewhat dangerous situation. For after all, what it has to say about truth and freedom and love—indeed, the whole of its teaching, its belief, its theory—may be nothing but human fantasy. Perhaps it is all a dream. Perhaps it is an attractive statement of what is most dreadfully and terribly *un-fact*. Perhaps it is a pretty lie. At best, perhaps, it is a guess—and it may, of course, be a true guess, but still a guess. Without some grounding in things as they are and as they have been, in history as it has happened, in human life as it has actually been lived, a religion could be a fairy tale and nothing else.

What is the one thing about Christianity which for these reasons is of enormous importance? It is the way in which the Christian creed or doctrine or belief, the Christian cult or devo-

tions of belonging, the Christian conduct or discipline or behavior, all find a center in history and in an historical human
life. I am talking, of course, about Jesus Christ and his absolute
centrality in Christianity.

On the lowest reckoning anyone can make about him, Jesus
was a real historical person who lived in this world at a particular
time and in a particular place, as all of us do. He can, in that
sense, be dated. That is the unique thing about facts: we can
assert a where and a when about them, as we cannot do of a fairy
story or a guess or a dream. Again, the impact which he made
on people who knew him and on successive human history has
been so tremendous that, as Emerson once put it, his name "is
not so much written as ploughed" into this world of ours. The
stories about him, which anybody can read in the book we call
the New Testament, make it perfectly plain to us that he stood
for truth, that he respected and treated men as free agents, and
that in his relationships with others he embodied a positive,
vigorous, out-going love. This is why the insistence that Christians have always made on truth, freedom, and love, is not accidental; it is all tied up with this Man and with what Christians
have believed about him.

What Christians have believed about him is the clue to the
whole Christian religion, as distinguished from every other religion. It can be put in a few very simple words. They have
believed that he is the person in whom, the place where, and the
time when, the *Truth* about God and about man and about the
world was made manifest to the human race. Whatever may
be the case elsewhere and otherwise, *this*, they have said, is
central and focal and decisive.

Could it be, then, that in this Man, more than in anybody else
or anywhere else, God—the great Reality who can fulfill and
complete us by giving us proportion, perspective, and power—
somehow got himself involved in our human affairs?—and to a

42

degree and with an intensity found nowhere else? Could it be that in him, as in nobody else and nowhere else, God dwells in human life? Could it be that, while he was a true and genuine man, there was working in him and acting through him the unseen being, the ultimate and basic Reality who in many different ways and in many differing degrees is working in and acting through all men, through all history, through all nature, through the whole world? Could he, among the sons of God, be *the* Son?

The whole Christian religion is built around an affirmative answer to these questions. It says "yes" to every one of them. It declares that God was in Christ. It declares that in him true God dwelt in a true man. It has been saying this from the very beginning. It keeps on saying it. And when it stops saying it, Christianity will no longer exist. All of the Christian creed or doctrine or belief, all of its cult or devotion or worship, all of its conduct or discipline or behavior, are simply the outgrowth and consequence of that one big basic affirmation. In that sense Christianity *is* Christ. And the fact of Christ, and the centrality thus given him in Christianity, is the one essential and inescapable difference between Christianity and all other religions. *He* is the difference.

It has been far from my intention to say that all of the non-Christian religions are entirely false. To say that would, I think, be sheer nonsense. On the contrary, there are good things in all of them. What I have been seeking to do is to show that some of the major assertions of these religions simply will not do. And these assertions are either true or false. The world cannot be both a true reality, as Judaism and Christianity declare, and at the same time a dream or illusion. On the other hand, if we believe—as I do— that God is always seeking to reveal something of himself to men; if we believe—as I do—that everybody to some degree and in some fashion responds to that effort on God's part, then every religion has at least something in it which helps people to know God and to get, in some way, help in finding proportion, perspective, and power from him. As a matter of fact, that is why nobody's situation is entirely hopeless and helpless. That is why we all have some glimmerings of a meaning in things, so that we manage to get along, however stumblingly and weakly.

Let me put down three points as a sort of summary of the position which seems to me reasonable in these matters—a position, incidentally, which the great main stream of Christian thought has consistently adopted, however some sectarians may at one time or another have failed to emphasize it. Here are the points:

1. It is part of Christian teaching that God "has nowhere left himself without witness." Hence everybody, in some way or other—and even when he does not consciously know what it is all about—is in some sort of touch with God. God is the one Reality from whom nobody can "play hooky." He is inescapable because he is absolutely basic. But he is in touch with people through all sorts of "incognitos" and he always is known to them and by them in the degree and fashion in which they can grasp what they do know about him. That goes for the religions of the world as well as for individual people.

2. It is part of Christian teaching that these glimpses, hints, contacts, moments of awareness of God are not *denied* but completed, and where necessary corrected, through what God did in Jesus Christ. So, to put it in the language of historical Christian thought, there is a "general revelation of God" and there is a "special revelation of God." In other words, there is a pervasive and diffused operation of God in nature, in history, and in the lives of men, and there is also a concentrated, focused,

peculiarly decisive operation of God in and through and by Jesus Christ.

3. It is not part of Christian teaching to assert that "the heathen in his blindness bows down to wood and stone." Those words, which occur in a familiar hymn, are completely and horribly *un*-Christian; they should be excised from the hymn and they should never be used by anybody who professes to hold what authentic historical Christianity has always centrally taught. Of course the heathen (the non-Christian) does not "bow down to wood and stone." He bows down to whatever little bit of God he may have met in the place where he is and under the circumstances by which he has been shaped. The job of the Christian is not to make fun of this, to deny its truth, or to reject its significance for that man; the job of the Christian is to show that the little bit of God he has met is enlarged and enriched, is corrected where it has been misleading or even partially false, and above all is crowned and completed when the "heathen" is brought to see God in Jesus Christ—Jesus Christ, who is "the desire of all nations."

4

DOESN'T SCIENCE ANSWER
OUR QUESTIONS?

SOME reader is likely to say: "What is the sense of cluttering things up with talk about religion? I know that man needs proportion and perspective and power. I know that in the past people have looked for these things from religion. But nowadays we have science. And science can tell us all we need to know and give us all we need to have."

There can be no doubt that a great many of our contemporaries do have that sort of idea. They know the great and wonderful things science has accomplished during the past century. The whole world is a different—if not a better—place because of scientific research, discovery and invention. We have learned much about the world, from the vastness of space to the tininess of the electron. We understand ourselves a great deal better, not only through the amazing discoveries made in chemistry and biology but also through the work of the psychologists and especially the "depth" psychologists like Freud and Jung. We seem to be conquering space, and already sensible people, not just dreamers, speak of our visiting other planets. Sputnik and Lutnik and the rest have opened up such possibilities for men.

Yes, science has done great things. And because of this, many of our contemporaries think there is absolutely no limit to what

47

science can do. They see no reason why it should not solve our personal problems, by the use of psychological techniques; our physical problems, by chemical and other therapeutic developments; our social and political problems, by the application of the knowledge gained through a study of sociological factors in human experience—and so on, and on, and on.

It is because there is such widespread confidence in what science can do that it is necessary for us to say something about this whole subject. What, in fact, can science tell us and what can it give us and do for us? And what, if any, are the things that science can neither know or give?

First of all, we ought to ask ourselves what science actually is. A simple definition of science is the study of things (including human beings) by the use of certain special methods. Those methods are essentially the application of the principles of precise observation and measurement. Sometimes this is done with the use of instruments which enlarge our human senses, widen their capacity to a tremendous extent, and bring into our range of observation aspects of the world which the naked eye, for example, can never contemplate. Sometimes the application is by the carrying out of experimental procedures in which reactions of one sort or another are carefully noted. Sometimes it is with statistical correlations of one set of data with another set of data, especially in the realm of sociology.

The result of such observation and measurement is the accumulation of an enormous mass of related materials which can be organized in specific patterns or interpreted through the use of specific categories. When this is done, what emerges are some general principles which are believed to cover a great many instances of behavior or action or reaction. The principles can be checked by further observation and experiment, to see how far they actually hold good when put to the test. If they appear to have a sufficiently wide application, if they cover with fair accuracy the whole field which is under study, then they are likely to be called "laws"—although nowadays scientists are a little hesitant in using this word, since what the scientists are talking about are not regulations that are, so to say, enforced by some authority, but rather are regularities that are known to have happened a great many times.

This is the way theoretical science proceeds. It is too bad that so many of our contemporaries do not bother much about this theoretical side of science or "basic science," as it is sometimes called. For most people it is the practical application of the theory, and the practical results in increasing power over this or that area of life or nature, which seem all important.

Of course, that is to put the cart before the horse. Our leading scientists are very conscious of this danger, and more and more the common man is coming to see that theory here, as elsewhere, has a great deal to do with practice. This explains the increasing emphasis in scientific schools, universities, and research centers, on "basic science" rather than on "applied science." In fact, some people have come to understand that the pursuit of truth about the way the world functions is a good thing in and of itself, quite apart from any results it may give us in manipulating the world for our own benefit—or to our own destruction, as seems to be the case with the application of some of the modern discoveries.

When a scientist talks in this fashion—about the value of knowledge for its own sake—he comes close to talking like a religious man. What he is saying is that there are some things that are good in themselves, that are worth knowing or having just because they are what they are. That is not far from saying, religiously, that there is Truth which man ought to know; that freedom to seek it is one of the things that distinguishes a man from a monkey; and that love of Truth is among the highest qualities known in human experience. Some of the greatest scientists, like Darwin and Huxley in the last century, and Einstein in this one, have in that sense really talked in a very religious manner about the work in which they were engaged.

Science is precise, systematic, controlled observation, experiment, and measurement, with the interpretation of the accumulated data in certain terms and by the use of certain types of explanation which seem appropriate to them. There have always been scientifically minded people in the world, evidently from the very earliest days of human history, but it is only during the past hundred years that the development of scientific procedures has gone so far that what sometimes looks like an almost inclusive picture of how the world works has been available. In that hundred years we have learned a vast amount about nearly everything—about nature, man, the way nature and man came to be, how they function, and how they apparently will function in any foreseeable future. This predictive aspect of science has been of great significance; for it has not only given us a picture of the world in which regularity and order seem the norm of things, but has also tended to suggest that novelty and change are hardly to be expected—not that the real scientists have talked that way, but rather that the ordinary man, without expert knowledge, has seemed to assume that this is so.

The fact is, however, that science as such can explain nothing. Let us be careful here. What I mean is that in the final analysis, science cannot tell us why things are, what they are here for, and where they are going. It can, and it does, report to us with eminent success how things are and how things behave, so far as observation and experiment can tell this. It is able to describe the way things work, the way they run, what they are made of, the direction which they seem to be taking so far as careful observation can find out. But what it cannot do, and what the greatest of scientists readily admit it cannot do, is tell us why anything really is, what are the purposes and values which in the last resort would be the only explanation that would really cover the ground, and where things are going in the final accounting of facts.

When a scientist begins to talk about matters like that, he is no longer talking as a scientist but as a man, and as a philosopher at that. Why is there a world at all? Why does it exist? What is it for? What purposes does it serve? These are questions everybody wants to have answered; but these are also questions which scientific procedures will not answer, since scientific procedures are set up and are employed to find out something else. Their purpose is to show linkages between what seem to be causes and what seem to be effects. But to show the linkages will not tell us why there are linkages. Science can tell us nearly everything about ourselves, for example, except for the one thing which above all else we want to know: what are we here for? what is, or what ought to be, the purpose of human life?

Is this strange creature called man, made up as he is of chemicals which can be described as working in this particular way, possessed as he is of those physiological and psychological and sociological ways of functioning which can be observed and reported, anything more than this? Does he count in the scheme of things? Is he only another bit of animality let loose in the world, or is he here for some other purpose? Who is he, anyway?

Science does not interest itself in these matters. Of course, as I have said, scientists themselves are bound to have some ideas, good or bad, false or true, on these things. But this is because a scientist is a man, before he is a scientist; and he continues to be a man, even when he is a scientist. So he has opinions on such matters. But we are no more obliged to pay attention to what he says about them, than we are obliged to bow low before the authority of the expert in any field when he talks about what is entirely outside that field.

I do not ask an expert engineer to tell me whether Bach is a greater composer than Beethoven. I do not ask my dentist to discover for me whether Raphael or Michelangelo is the better painter. I ought not to turn to Dr. Einstein for information on the nature of God; and when that distinguished expert once permitted himself to deny that God is "personal," his opinion on the subject was of no more value than the opinion of the humblest ignorant peasant who in his own way may have reached an entirely different conclusion.

These big ultimate questions of *why* are really the questions of meaning and purpose and value. Such questions belong in the realm of philosophy, not in the realm of science. The philosopher is the man who ought to deal with them, for he is specially trained to consider the significance of problems of this sort. His job is to take into account a great deal more than the scientific knowledge which we have been able to acquire. He must consider what art and poetry have to say; he must listen to what can be heard from every other interest that has engaged man's attention; he must look at what principles of human conduct have developed and what ground they may have in experience; he must even pay heed to the saints, the religious men and women of the ages, the simple folk who have lived in the conviction that their lives have point and significance. There is much in human experience which escapes precise scientific observation; and it is with this additional material that the philosopher also concerns himself. If he confined his attention to scientific data alone, that would mean that he was not taking account of all the facts there are.

A good example of the failure of science to give a full report may be found in the well-known Kinsey reports on sexual behavior in American men and women. Dr. Kinsey and his colleagues set out to discover, by the use of questionaires, exactly how men and women in the United States behave in matters of sexual activity. He listed a variety of "sexual outlets"; he arranged his material in terms of them; and he was able to show that this and that fact concerning behavior may be regarded as established. What he did not do and what he could not do, was to show anything at all about the meaning of human love. He could not determine the degree to which self-giving and faithful devotion to another person is related to the "sexual outlets." Above all, he could not describe what we might call the feeling a lover has when he seeks the closest possible union with the person he loves. Nor could he say, in terms of his own classifications, whether love is the key to the very heart of reality itself— whether we may take the human experience of utter devotion to the beloved one as the clue to the nature of God so that it is not nonsense but the highest truth to affirm that "God is love."

In our own experience we all know this to be the case. We all know that scientific observation and experiment will not give us information on these matters. Nobody deeply in love believes that a precise report on his beloved's anatomical structure, chemical constituents, biological drives, psychological determinants, and social relationships, will tell him the whole story about her. There is much, much more than that. There is the girl herself, with her unique personality, the meaning which she has for him, and the meaning which she has in herself. We cannot exhaustively and completely explain anything or anyone by the application of scientific tests and the making of scientific observations and experiments; we cannot even satisfactorily describe, in the full sense, although we may come fairly close to an accurate behavioral description.

In this example we have what the experts in logic would call a paradigm or model for all experience and the whole of human enterprise. Not only in human love, but in appreciation of beauty, regard for truth, pursuit of goodness, concern for justice, seeking for meaning, relationship to God, the same holds true. We do not deny the tremendous importance of science when we recognize that it is not a total story of all that has been, is, and will be.

Obviously science is not a useless pursuit. We have learned so much about our world, about things in it, and about ourselves, through the use of scientific methods, that we should be fools, and dangerous fools, if we disregarded it. What I am suggesting, however, is that there is all the difference in the world between saying: "These things are true, so far as we can see, and we must pay the closest attention to them. And yet, and yet, there is something more . . ." and saying, "*Nothing* but these things is true . . ."

I have often thought one of the indications that a man is really living at the deepest level and is aware of the highest possibilities, is simply whether his way of seeing is of the "nothing but" sort or is of the "how much more" sort. The man who sees things in the latter fashion is the man who is open, generous, able to grow and develop; while the former kind of man is all too likely to be narrow, inhospitable, and confined to his own little set of ideas and opinions. The wise man is the man who knows that science can tell us a great deal, but who also knows that a great deal (and the most important things in life are included in this "great deal") escapes science and that there is much with which science is not competent to deal.

One of the tragedies in the relationship of scientific methods and discoveries on the one hand, and the religious attitude and experience on the other, has been that both sides have sometimes forgotten what I have just been suggesting. Some scientists, but also a great many more people who have been deeply and rightly impressed by scientific discoveries, have had a tendency to talk as if they thought that what science tells us is all there is to know. Religious people, on their part, have tended to reject much of science because they were so sure that they themselves had all the answers. The truth is that each needs the other—science to

54

tell us how things run, religion to tell us what they run for; science to give us observational and experimental reports and descriptions, religion to help us reach the answer to the great questions of why and to what purpose or end.

Once again, science as such is entirely unable to tell us how we ought to answer the moral question, whether this or that is right or wrong, good or bad. In our own time, the atomic scientists have come to realize this. They know that they can split the atom and release its incredible power. But the power which they can release is power for human destruction or power for human development. Science, in itself, cannot say which of the two uses is the right one. That is why many atomic scientists have united in a group whose chief concern is to deal with such problems; that is why they ask for the contributions of men and women in other than scientific fields, to assist them in working, as men, toward an answer to this frightful and pressing problem, upon which hangs the future of the human race. Great men in this field, like Dr. Urey and Dr. Oppenheimer, have expressed over and over again their deep concern about these matters.

Practically speaking, as we have seen, science gives us much that we need and value. It gives the knowledge and the tools with which we can work to accomplish many great goals. But it cannot establish for us the final goals which make sense of all the smaller ones along the road. It cannot tell us what the whole business means; it cannot give us what teenagers a few years ago used to call "the big picture." We must get that information somewhere else. Science can tell us a great deal about the stuff of which we are made, but it cannot tell us what we are to make of that stuff. We must get that information elsewhere. Science can tell us, with fair accuracy, how the world runs and it can trace the development of the world from star-dust to man's "unconquerable mind." But it cannot tell us whether there is any purpose in the whole show, nor can it give us information about what that purpose is. We must get that information from another kind of activity, if we are to get it at all.

This is why I dared to say that science cannot tell us what above all else we need to know, nor can it give us what above all else we need to have. It can do a lot; it has done a lot in the past and it promises to do a lot in the future. We ought to be grateful for what it offers us. But it cannot do everything. And to put the point very frankly and very plainly, the man who assumes that it can is fooling himself—and in doing that, he is likely to be a pretty limited sort of man.

On the other hand, religion must take account of all that science has discovered. No religious faith which denies this or which tries to minimize its importance, however limited that may be, will be of much use to people living in the twentieth century. There is no doubt that science has changed our world-picture enormously. People who refuse to accept that change are people who are trying to live in a day which is past and done with; they are not living in the world of today.

Science is so important that a religion which disregards it is as good as dead. But it is not so important that it can supply us with all we need. Above all it cannot help us solve the problem of "what, if anything, is the matter with *me?*"

5

IS ANYTHING THE MATTER
WITH MAN?

WE began this book with a description of the way in which so many of us today feel an almost indefinable dis-ease or disquietude—a sense of quiet desperation. We saw that this awareness, while not with us all the time, comes now and again in the moments when things seem to go wrong and when life appears to be "messed-up." There is a consciousness of maladjustment which leads to a sense of loneliness and lostness.

The cause is the unpleasant but very real fact of *sin*.

Probably there are few words which have been so unpopular in recent years. Many people are likely to think of sin in connection with deadly dull pietists who spend their time criticizing the fun of others, and who go around nosing out what they think is wrong with their friends, sometimes manufacturing wrongs out of what really are "rights."

I wish that we could have some other word than "sin" to describe the real facts to which it points and which it is intended to describe, so that we should no longer be obliged to use a term that has become meaningless and silly for a great many of our contemporaries. However, we seem to be "stuck" with the word, for nobody has managed yet to find another which so satisfactorily denotes what is meant. And it is obvious that whether we like it or not we are certainly "stuck" with what sin denotes.

57

It is important that we forget, if we can, all the silly and pica-yune notions about the meaning of sin which the "goody-goodies" and the "blue-noses" may have had in mind. What we want to do here is to get at the whole business by looking at the facts and seeing what we can make of them.

Man feels homeless; he feels lost and lonely; he has a sense of disquietude springing from quiet desperation. He feels a dis-ease about himself and about his relationship to the world in which he is placed. That there is such an experience nobody can deny. But deep down, underneath this dissatisfaction and desperation, there is something else which now and again comes up to con-sciousness—and which is always there, as a kind of pervasive awareness which accompanies all human living when it is not reduced to the level of sheer animality. This is a feeling that we are not what we ought to be. We are not what we were made to be. And we are in some fashion responsible for this failure.

Not only do people have a disagreeable consciousness that the world is a "messed-up" world. When they are really themselves, in moments when they are alone and can for a little time *look* at themselves, they have an even more disagreeable consciousness that they themselves are "messed-up" too. We know the phrase that was used a few years back to describe an adolescent who was in serious emotional difficulties: he was called "a crazy, mixed-up kid." Actually, it would seem to be the disagreeable fact that this phrase describes, in at least the word "mixed-up," not only the teen-ager in his confusion and bewilderment, with all his problems of growing-up emotionally; it also describes something about every son of man. We are "mixed-up"; and the reason that we are "mixed-up" is that we are "messed-up."

For most of us this situation is not present in any aggravated form. And, of course, it is not usually an obvious situation. We look and we act, and, a good deal of the time, we feel like normal, respectable, moderately happy people. Very likely we do not do anything socially reprehensible. We don't drink too much, or at any rate we don't do it very often. We don't run around with somebody else's wife. We have never stolen any money. We pay our bills, we vote at election time, we live decently and try to be friendly with our neighbors and act like a good citizen. Sure enough!

But there is something deeper than that. Which of us could honestly say that he is living up to the full limits of his human capacity? Which of us could say that he is in complete charity and understanding with others? Which of us is not envious, even if only very slightly, of the good fortune of our friends? Which of us does not have, hidden somewhere in a dark closet of his memory, a deed, a word, a thought, of which he is honestly ashamed when he has the courage to take it out and look at it?

The fact is, then, that everybody knows, when he is really being honest and not engaging in the pleasant game of deluding himself about himself, that he has "done the things which he ought not to have done, and left undone the things which he ought to have done." Not all the time, not in every instance, but at *this* point and in *that* way, we have failed to be our true and intentional selves. And it is, perhaps, especially true that while it is not always easy to see what it is that we have done that is "wrong" for a person with our possibilities and capacities to do, it is fairly easy to see that there are a great many things left undone which we could have done, should have done, and even would have done, if we had "got around to it" or felt that it was within the range of our interests to do them.

Nobody, and particularly the best of us, would really claim to be a plaster saint; but it is equally true that each of us has been less than a true, full, "honest-to-God" man or woman. For the point of the whole business is that we have failed to be truly human. If we believe in God, we should see that God's will for us, above all else, is that we be what we are. We are men; what we ought to be is men in the complete sense of that word. And we have not been this because we have in one way or another, responsibly and knowingly, failed ourselves. And that means that we have also failed God.

It does not at all help to say that it is not our fault, that we never had the breaks, that the dice were loaded against us. As a matter of fact, we know very well, when we engage in honest self-examination, that most talk of that sort is sheer claptrap. Probably we did not have all the chances we might have had or should have liked to have; very likely there were plenty of obstacles in our way. Yet, in the depth of an honest self-examination, we know that (granted our "bad luck") we have not done what we might have done and that we have left undone what we could perfectly well have done—and that this is so time after time, case after case, instance after instance.

One of our difficulties is that we do not often enough engage in such honest self-examination. Socrates said that "the unexamined life is not worth living." What he meant was that a man is in this respect different from the animals; he can look at himself, examine himself, see what he is and where he is, what he has been and what he has done. Cows, monkeys, pigs, and laughing-jackasses do not do this sort of thing; man can do it—and Socrates believed that if a man does not, then he is a pretty poor sort of man.

When I look at myself in this fashion, I know that all I have been saying in the above paragraphs is true of me. Somehow I have the certainty that it is true of everybody else, too. It is a poor excuse when we have to try to weasel out of responsibility and blame society or our neighbors or our parents or our employers or our wife or husband, or anybody else we may happen to think of, in the desperate effort to free ourselves from what we know very well indeed. We are not what we ought to be.

We are not what we could be. And there is no honest escape from that fact.

The recognition that this is so will go a long way to help us understand what the great religions, and especially Christianity, are talking about when they use a word like "sin" and insist that a basic human need is deliverance from sin.

Jesus said that he had not come to "seek for" the "righteous" —the people who thought they were quite all right, who believed themselves to be pretty good people, who felt that they did not need any help. He had come, he said, to "seek for" the "sinners" —the people who could not brag about their virtues, who knew they were not "pretty good," who honestly saw that they had disgraced their manhood by acting like something less than a man, and who therefore knew that they needed help.

Of course, the irony of his statement lies in the truth that it is precisely the people who think themselves righteous who are in the worst situation; these people are guilty of what Plato called "the lie in the soul," for they are fooling themselves. As modern psychological analysis has made so plain to us, they are putting up a screen or defense mechanism by which they attempt to evade the real and ugly facts about themselves.

All this gives us our clue to the meaning of the word "sin." Sin is not some peculiar little idea that religious people like to play around with. It is a word that seeks to describe a fact nobody can avoid or evade; sin is a characteristic of every human life known to us, save One alone. It is a word used to point to the terribly tragic, but terribly real, truth. We, who are men "made in the image of God" and intended to live the full, rich, free, abundant, dynamic life which is proper to manhood, are in actuality those who distort that image and live narrow, confined, poor, static, sometimes cheap, little lives. We "want what we want when we want it," as a song of the early 'twenties put it, and we do not think to ask whether it is good for us, whether it helps us to become true men, whether it promotes the well-being of others and of the whole world. We just "want" it, and so we act upon our uncriticized desire.

Have you ever thought about the words we commonly use to describe the kinds of people we do not like? We call them "dogs" or "cats" or "snakes" or "jackasses" or "wolves" or "tigers"—and by using these words about them, we really intend to say that although they are human beings they are acting as if they were more or less like the animals we mention to describe them. Now nobody would blame a dog for acting like a dog, or a cat for acting like a cat, or a snake for acting like a snake. That is their nature; and as a matter of fact, they are on the whole doing the right thing for them when they act as they do. But when we see a man whose character and behavior is "slinky," we do not like it. We are repelled. Of course, cats are not really "slinky"; that is a human reading of their ways. But the point is clear enough. They seem to us to act in a way that is not human; and when men act in a way that is not human, we feel disturbed.

Man is the only creature to whom you can meaningfully say, "Be a man." G. K. Chesterton pointed this out years ago. As he remarked, it would be silly to tell some animal to be himself, for he already is being himself to the limit of his ability. A dog is being a dog to the limit of his "dogginess"; a snake is being a snake to the limit of his "snakeship." But what man is there who can honestly say that he is being a man to the limit of his manhood? And we can tell a man that he is failing in this respect, just as we can recognize that the same thing is true of ourselves.

This is just another way of saying there is something not right about us. Of course it is much easier for us to see this—or so we think, anyway—in other people. It is especially easy to see it in the people with whom we spend much of our time. However, these people could quite readily say the same thing about us, too. The basic truth here is that whether we admit it to ourselves, or whether we try to fool ourselves about how wonderful we are, we are disloyal to the possibilities with which we have been endowed. We distort the image of God in us. In other words, we are "sinners."

I do not wish to suggest that we should be obsessed by this fact. Obsession by our sin is not healthy, for it means that we spend so much time in thinking how bad we are that we never have time to recognize the possibility that something good can be made of us. I am not pleading for an obsession with—a constant dwelling upon, and a sort of perverted delight in—our failure to be true men. There is nothing whatsoever to be said for what somebody once called a vermiform ("worm's-eye") attitude to life. I am pleading for an honest recognition of something that I know to be true of myself and that I am certain is true of other people too. I am asking that we shall honestly make an avowal of the fact. We need not go around telling other people what terrible sinners we are. They probably know it already anyway, but have not bothered to tell us. What we do need is to know it for ourselves and to acknowledge it to ourselves. In a word, we need to be honest people—honest about ourselves.

It is this kind of experienced awareness that religion, and especially the Christian religion, is talking about when it puts such an emphasis on man's sin and on the necessity of doing something about it. For Christianity, the very first step in mature living is to be as honest as one can, to face realities as they are.

From its earliest days, Christianity has been strongly insistent on the reality of sin in the lives of men and women and children, however veiled that sin may be and however we may hope to hide it from ourselves and from others. So strong has been this insistence that now and again great Christian thinkers, contemplating, as they did, their own experience, have tended to fall into dangerous sin-obsession. St. Augustine is a case in point and there have been many others. But we ought not to condemn their excesses in statement, without at least first recognizing that they were talking about something very real. Perhaps a measure of their greatness is that even though they did thus exaggerate their sin, they were at the very least trying to be honest about themselves and about the need which they felt for what they called "redemption."

When you get underneath all the padding, all the evasion, all the surface fraud, there is a fact which is unmistakable and unescapable. That fact is that we are less than we were meant to be, less than we could be, less than we should be. Each of us has his own special way of being less than a man. Nobody is exactly like anybody else; each of us is himself. Each of us has his own particular way of distorting the image of God. It is likely that this will be in terms of the actual possibilities that are offered to us by life; these will determine the situations and the conditions under which we deny our manhood, and they will also determine the particular lines along which we act in denying it. But we are all in the same boat in the one big thing: that is, we are all distorters of the divine image in us, all deniers of our manhood, all ready to take the easier way and avoid the hard road to full and complete human life.

When we say that sin is a rejection of God's will, this is what we mean. It is not as if God were an arbitrary and tyrannical dictator who had established a set of laws which men would inevitably break and disobey if they were to live at all. On the contrary, God has made us to be men and to be men to the limit of our human possibility. *That* is his will for us; *that* is his law: the law of full, true, genuine, complete manhood. When we

64

fail to be ourselves as we are meant to be, to be men, to seek to live like men in the full, responsible, and true sense of that word, what we are then doing is obviously rejecting his law, disobeying his will, flouting him and his purpose for his human children.

If that is the fact, certainly we all need to have help. We need to have "salvation"—which is just another, and a religious, way of saying that we need to have health. The need is, or should be, perfectly obvious, once we see ourselves as we are.

There is still another thing about which we should be clear in our minds. We are all in this together. It is not just that you and I, as individuals, act like less than men, think like less than men, and so are less than men. We affect one another. What each one of us says and thinks and does goes out from us, and in some strange and terrifying way harms other people. It does that in some pretty obvious ways, as when a gossip succeeds in wrecking the free and easy companionship of a group with whom he spends much of his time. It does it when words and deeds of hatred and distrust bring about the situations which ultimately can lead to war. But it does it, too, in more subtle and obscure ways, as when our attitude of unspoken distrust and suspicion communicates itself in a mysterious manner to other people and thus brings about a disintegration and perversion of other lives—very often the lives of those with whom we most intimately are related—and does it as readily, and as horribly, as spoken words and visible actions.

This has been going on for hundreds and thousands of years. Is it any wonder then, that human society is the way it is? All the accumulated resentments, envyings, jealousies, hatreds, lusts, lies, meannesses, cheapnesses, stealings, libelings, slanders, gossiping, and the like—the distrusts and suspicions, the mistrusts and the misrepresentations—have not just passed away into the void. In the wonderful linkage of cause and effect, in the orderly and constant movement of human lives through the ages, these things have got hold of succeeding generations of men and women. We simply cannot escape, even when we stupidly try to deny or evade, this terrible reality.

It is of the mercy of God that we are not in a worse state than in fact we are. In countless ways he is at work to absorb and reduce this mass of human evil, of sin and false manhood. Subtly, but none the less surely, he counteracts evil with good. That is one of the ways in which we can most readily recognize him in the world of men. Whenever and wherever there are helping, healing, health-giving influences, there God is at work, sometimes in most unexpected places and in most surprising people. Christian faith dares to affirm that God is thus persistently active in his world, although his activity is under an incognito, doing just this sort of thing, so that he can bring the whole of his creation and especially his human children to a fuller conformity with his plan and purpose and will.

But there is still something more to be said. This time it is more cheerful. Christianity, at any rate, cannot be a religion of gloom. It recognizes and insists upon the reality of human sin; it see that not only individual men and women, but the society which they compose and of which they are composed, is far from what it should be. But it goes on to say that the last word is with God, who loves men and helps them.

St. Augustine, addressing God in the first sentence of his autobiographical work, *The Confessions*, says, "Thou has made us for thyself"—or, as it should be translated, "toward thee." Here is a recognition that man is by nature, by what he was created for, "turned to God" and made for fulfillment because in God he can be complete and whole. Then St. Augustine goes on in the same sentence, to say this: "And our heart is restless"—the Latin word means "unquiet" or "disturbed"—"until it rests in thee." That expresses the disquietude, dis-ease, about which we have spoken—the thing which underlies the sense of quiet desperation which men know so well.

Why then do we have this disquietude? Because we were created for one purpose, which undergirds and explains all the lesser purposes of our human existence. We were made to respond in full and complete manhood to God. The purpose of human life is that each of us, and all of us together, should be a man with other men, compact of body and mind and will and heart, living richly and healthily with others, looking toward God as the integrating center of our human existence and finding in our relationship with him a meaning and a dignity and a purpose and a worth which will redeem our little lives from triviality and stupidity, from despair and frustration, from distortion and degradation.

When we look, not at our dis-ease, but at our disease, we find that our sickness comes from our willful desire to run the show for ourselves and by ourselves. This is the explanation of our sin; this is the reason for our "less-than-manhood." We forget that God is the integrating center and we claim that we are—or at least we act on that unspoken claim. Is it then any wonder that our lives are messed-up and that we ourselves are mixed-up? How could it be otherwise? For God is at the center and God is the center of things. To act and think as if it were otherwise, as if we were the "big boss," will inevitably put the whole picture in the wrong perspective, deprive us of a right proportion in all things, and so mix us up and mess us up that the power for right living simply cannot get to us.

Yet God has made us for himself. That means that our sin is not the last word. God's acceptance of us, his willingness and his ability to help us, his love for us, is bigger and much more important than our sin. That, above all, is why we need not be, and ought not be, obsessed by our sin. We are "made in his image"—that is, we are reflections of God on a small scale, intended to show his love and his loveliness in our lives, and to make his goodness and truth known in our own human realm as the men he wants us to be.

And what is the most wonderful thing of all in the Christian claim, is that once, in the history of men and through the governing work of God in the affairs of his world, the Image of God in which we are made was fully manifested, embodied, expressed in a full, complete, true human life. We are indeed "made in God's image," but we have distorted and dirtied it. Jesus Christ, a Brother Man who lived as we do in this world of human affairs, is the *express* and the *expressed* Image of God—and Christianity makes bold to proclaim that as he is, so may we be, through the grace and power which comes to us from him.

6

HOW CAN CHRIST HELP US?

It is the Christian claim, as we indicated, that Jesus Christ can and does do something to help man.

Perhaps we can best arrive at the answer to how He does so by approaching it from a tangent. Man knows both his dis-ease and his disease; what he needs is some resting-place or abiding certainty which will counter the dis-ease. To counter the dis-ease, he needs healing or restoration to full healthy manhood. He needs the former if he is to become a completed, fulfilled man; he needs the latter if he is to recover from his inordination, his mixed-up and messed-up condition. The problem is where to get these things and how to get them.

You cannot do this yourself simply by some kind of psychological exercises. The trouble with attempts of that sort is that they fail us when we are really up against life. Nobody can fool himself forever; somehow or other the facts will find him out. It is impossible to attempt, by saying over and over again that everything is all right, to extricate oneself; the time will come when even the ostrich must take his head out of the sand.

This truth, that we are not able by some kind of psychological legerdemain to fix things up for ourselves, is evidence of something extremely important for us to know—that we depend always upon our environment, upon what goes on outside us, for our full self-realization. Many people go wrong here. They seem to think that if only they were let alone, or would let other people alone, they could take care of themselves. But life cannot be lived that way, at any level. We belong to each other, for better or for worse; our very existence consists largely in our relationship with other people. What is more, our existence consists also in our relationship to the bigger environment—to the whole world of things and stuff, to the values or ideals whatever they are which run through the whole creation, to the power which moves things along and makes things grow, and above all to the God from whom that power derives and who is the final environment of man.

Martin Luther has a very illuminating phrase to describe the human predicament. He says that man is "twisted in on himself"—the Latin phrase he used was *incurvatus in se*. We go round in circles, with ourselves as the pretended center.

In the New Testament, St. Peter is represented as preaching one of the first Christian sermons, and in it he tells those who hear him that they belong to a generation that is *skolias*. That is a Greek word which our Authorized Version of the Bible translates as "untoward," but which actually means just about what Luther said; it means "going round in circles." We are like squirrels in a squirrel-cage; we go round and round, but like the squirrels we never get anywhere. The same thing is true when we look at our wishes and desires.

The poet W. H. Auden has said that "the desires of the heart are crooked as corkscrews." They are, because our hearts are like corkscrews; round and round they turn, but unlike a real corkscrew, they are not able to open any bottles which will give us the wine of life. What is needed is help from somewhere else.

One of the most remarkable phenomena of our time is the enormous number of people who are turning for help to somebody not themselves—in this instance to the psychiatrists and the psychoanalysts. They see the need to bring their troubles to another person, who supposedly has expert knowledge and the ability to help them. And they are able to get such help, in very large degree. Yet many of the most competent psychiatrists and psychoanalysts not only admit but willingly affirm that they are not competent to handle men's ultimate *spiritual* problems. They can do a fairly effective job with emotional disorders; but when these have been cleared away and people still remain uneasy and troubled in heart, something more is needed. When the guilt-complex has been removed the patient may still find that he feels guilty; and the reason for that can perfectly well be that in fact he *is* guilty.

Many people turn to a friend for consolation and strengthening. They succeed thus in extroverting themselves, as the psychologists would say, and this is a basic need of men. To stop being completely introverted about one's difficulties, to get attached somehow or other to what is not ourselves, will give us a hold on reality which steadies our lives. Best of all, if we feel that a hand is reached out to us we have a deep sense of gratitude for a rescue which we know we needed.

We should not think that God is far away outside the world and only now and again comes crashing in to help us when matters get to an impasse. We should not think that he does this in our own lives. For the truth is that God is always here, right in this world and close at hand; otherwise there would not be a world at all. It is God's ceaseless energizing, his constant presence and action, which holds the world in existence.

Our trouble is that we have blinded our eyes and stopped our ears, so that we fail to recognize him, and hence cannot turn to him and let him help us as he wishes. He is helping us all the time, anyway. He prevents things from being any worse than they are and he brings good out of the evil which we do, in quite surprising and unexpected ways. But because of the rights of men and the freedom which he has given them, he does not treat them as if they were puppets or manikins. He wants men to be men, which means that he wants them freely to respond to him, willingly to accept his help, and to do this of their own accord. He wants them to turn to him and let him give them his strength and his grace.

Though he is here all the time, there are certain times when he makes himself known through some especially vivid and intensive action. It is like the relationship between two friends. John is always there; he is always ready to help; he wants to be counted on. But until Fred, on his own account and for himself, recognizes and accepts the fact, the relationship is not all that it might be. Sometimes the only way in which Fred can be made to recognize and accept the fact, is for John to go out of his way, as we put it, to do some really striking thing which will wake Fred up to see the truth of the situation. John may say a word just when it is needed; he may do something like coming over to see Fred at a time when Fred least expects a visit; he may quietly fix something up so that Fred learns, perhaps to his surprise, that he has always been surrounded by the affection and concern of his friend. And that recognition on Fred's part, in response to John's word or action, changes the whole situation from then on.

God is always giving us strength and help. He is ever pressing into our lives. But he is doing this so constantly and uninterruptedly that we are quite likely to forget it or maybe never even to recognize it for what it is. If he is to change the situation, so that it is different from then on, he must do something in particular, not simply continue acting in general. This is what Christians have in mind when they believe that in one place God has acted with singular intensity, not by contradicting or denying the conditions of human life, but by getting involved in them with a completeness and directness which brings him vividly and strikingly before our eyes. This, Christians say, is the meaning of Jesus Christ.

And so we have come, by an oblique route, to the question which is the title of this chapter: "How can Christ help us?"

First of all, he lived a complete and full human life, showing what it really means to be a man. Explain it how you will, millions and millions of people, when they read the account of Jesus in the New Testament or hear it told by someone, feel convinced that in this life manhood is shown for what it really can be, for what it really is meant to be.

I do not wish to suggest that Jesus was a kind of walking encyclopedia or that he shared in every conceivable sort of human experience. Of course he did not; and if he had, he would not have been truly human at all. For the condition of manhood is to live in a particular time, at a particular place, under particular circumstances. There is no such thing as manhood in the abstract; manhood is always concrete and particular. What does mark the human life of Jesus Christ is a spirit or quality which in his own historical time and in his own local place both represents and expresses what man is when he is at his most complete.

That spirit might be characterized by two words. One is "love"—the positive, active, outgoing goodness manifested in a deep concern for others. The second word is "obedience"—and by this I mean the sonly or filial obedience which rejoices in doing the will of the Father, however difficult that will may seem to be. Both love and filial obedience are capable of an infinite variety of expressions, in different times and at different places.

So if we catch the spirit of Jesus, in this sense, we have got hold of the secret of human life. It is intended to be a life of love and filial obedience, and that is the way to fullness and completeness.

"Behold the Man," we read in the gospel of St. John. When we look at Jesus we see in him the truth about manhood. Of

73

course, though, that works both ways. It shows us what manhood really is; and it also makes us deeply conscious of what poor specimens of manhood each of us is, in comparison with this true manhood in Jesus. But not only does Jesus show us true manhood—and in showing it make us see ourselves as we are—he also gives us, through his capacity to influence our lives, the help we need if we are to grow toward true manhood. If he is like that, then we too can be like that. This would be a counsel of despair were it not for the fact that his influence—the Church calls it his "grace"—can work in us to make us be like him.

The way in which this has been described in Christian thinking in that when we make an act of commitment to him, surrendering our lives to him as our Master and our Lord, we are redeemed by his grace. His life gets into ours and begins to work upon it.

Human relationships will again help us to understand this. We know that it is possible for one person to influence another so deeply that he actually changes the other's character and makes him a new man. Somebody whom we admire not only provides us with a model to imitate; he also gives us, in some very strange and subtle way, something of himself which gets aboard our own ship of life and actually alters us.

So it is with Jesus. But there is a deeper truth here. For if the Christian claim be true, then Jesus is not only the true man and the giver of strength so that we can come to be like him. He is also—and this is the supremely important thing about him—the One in whom God himself is specially and decisively present and active, so far as human society and the human race are concerned. Hence the help he gives us is not just human assistance; it comes to us through Jesus' human life to be sure, but it comes to us from God. This is God's giving us the express image of manhood as it is meant to be, and it is God's giving us the grace

74

—the strength, the power, the freely bestowed help and favor— which will bring us to health and completeness.

Now, of course, every bit of assistance we get, even from our human friends, is always God's doing, in and through and by their human life and character and influence. But here in Jesus Christ God is at work to help us, with a directness and an intensity found nowhere else.

Perhaps we have all played with a reading-glass when we were children. We went out into the sunshine with the glass and twisted it and turned it in our hand. The rays of the sun were shining down everywhere; they were giving life and health, making the grass and flowers grow, warming and invigorating people who were walking around the garden. But when we managed to catch those rays in the glass so that they were focused, they had a new intensity. Then, if we put a piece of paper or cloth under them, they would set it on fire. In something of the same way, the focusing and intensifying of God's love and light and life in the human life of Jesus can set fire to the lives of those who are exposed to him. It is the fire of love, of life, and of light; and it burns away our selfishness and meanness and arrogance and all the rest of the evils that make us less than true men.

Furthermore, not only is Jesus the image of our true manhood. He is also the express Image of God in our manhood. It is important that we see that in and under the conditions which we know so well God is active on our behalf. Christianity is itself only when this conviction is central to it. Anything less than this would not be Christianity at all, but a poor substitute.

Now all that Jesus does is summed up in the Cross on which he died. The Cross, all by itself, would not mean anything. But the Cross, seen as summing up the whole of Jesus' life of love and filial obedience, placards before us the way of our "redemption." It *is* that way. Jesus dedicated his human life in commitment to

God and for the good of other men. The Cross concentrates that dedication.

A saint of the middle ages put this in simple words: "It is not the death, but the will of the One who died, which makes the Cross a sacrifice." St. Bernard, who said that, made clear that the death in itself would prove nothing; but that the willingness of Jesus to die in accordance with his dedication to the will of God, turns the death into the means whereby we see deep into the heart of the Crucified and can respond with grateful surrender to the love which brought him to that hill outside the walls of Jerusalem.

The life of Jesus did not end on the Cross. It was only the beginning. The experience of the first Christians makes this plain. However we may choose to explain the details of the story, those disciples knew with absolute certainty that Jesus Christ rose from the dead and was alive with them as a presence and power that made them, in their own words, "a new creation."

This means that they had the assurance, generated from their experience of his continuing presence and power among them, that Jesus' life and his willingness to die had been both validated and vindicated by God. He was risen—he was risen from the dead in the lives of his disciples, and he was risen from the dead so that in the full integrity of his personality he lived with God. Living with God, he was yet still with his disciples and with all others who committed themselves to him, who accepted him as their Master and Lord, and who found him the way to the truth about God and man and about their real relationship with one another.

Thus the way in which Christ can help us is like this. When I know that I cannot get out of the "jam" by myself, when I know that by myself I cannot reach complete manhood, I am not to try to run away from the facts, nor am I to think that by some trick I can escape their full impact. I must accept them as they are, for what they are. Then I can turn to Jesus Christ. I can steadily center my life on him; I can take him for my Master and Lord; I can open myself to receive from him, through a full response on my part, the strength that he can give; I can let God get at me through Jesus' life and death. God has validated and vindicated Jesus by raising him from the dead. That validation and vindication can be worked out in my life. Above all, I can seek to be in continuing and constant fellowship with him, through prayer and through the sacramental means which he has left for us all. That is how he can help me.

It is not going to happen in an instant. Like everything else worth while, it will take time. The theologians have a way of putting this. They tell us that while we are "justified"—set right with God—so soon as in faith we turn to Christ, still our "sanctification"—the working out of this in our experience so that we become like him, in complete and full manhood—is for the whole of our lifetime. The old tendencies, desires, self-willings, prides, do not die at once. They must be continually mortified or put to death by the new principle of Christ-life that is now in us.

Christ must grow in our own lives; and the growth will doubtless be pretty slow for most of us. But the principle has been established; the new life has been planted; the beginning has been made—and in a way that is the most important part of the story. The rest of the story is our own continual and constant willingness to be made over, to become what we were meant to be. And that, as T. S. Eliot tells us in *Four Quartets*, "is the work of a lifetime." But that is all right, for "Christ in us" is our hope of glory.

Sometimes we wonder about people who have not had the opportunity to hear of Christ, who have not been exposed to his influence, or who for some good reason (as they think) are unable to accept him. Some of us raise this as an objection to everything that has been said in the preceding pages. If a man or woman who has not heard of Christ, who has not been exposed to his influence, or who simply cannot accept him, is going to be damned, then God would appear to be a very mean and arbitrary being. As I have heard it said, "I can't believe in a God who damns people because they do not believe in somebody of whom they may never even have heard."

This problem, while often posed in perfectly good faith, rests on a misunderstanding which Christian people sometimes have augmented rather than corrected. The facts, however, are different.

The position which the great central stream of Christian thought has consistently adopted is that God is the kind of God who lived and worked in Jesus Christ; he is, indeed, "the God and Father of our Lord Jesus Christ." Since this is so, we can trust him to be more than fair; we can trust him to be unfailing in his love and understanding. As to people in the category we have been describing, he understands them and their situation. He will not refuse to give them whatever they are able to receive, now in this present life, and again in life beyond the grave. He can take their slightest action of good-will, their smallest devotion to the truth, their dedication to whatever has won their hearts, and he can use that as a starting-point for their growth towards him. How this can be done we do not know. That is God's business, not ours. We can—and indeed we must—leave such people in God's hands, as we must leave ourselves in those same hands. And to be in God's hands is the safest and best place to be.

This does not exempt us from working to share with as many people as we possibly can reach the wonder and the glory of new life which we have received from God through Christ. That is why Christians want to convert others, not in order to save them from eternal damnation, but because they want to share with those others something that they themselves have received. They want all men to know what St. Paul described as the "joy and peace" which comes from "believing" in Christ, in living in and with God, known and loved and served in his Son the Lord Jesus.

Furthermore, the life and death and the rising-again of Jesus Christ has made a difference in the whole structure of reality, in the way things actually are. Nowadays we know that the slightest change, the least occurrence in the order of nature has effects which reach to the farthest realms of space. The whole world is so closely knit, so organic, as the philosophers say, that you cannot lift a stone without some result (however infinitesimal it may be) on the remotest planet. If this is true of physical reality, it is even more true of things spiritual. Any act or deed or thought or word of ours has effects which spread out to the whole range of life. They are like the ripples which are caused when a stone is thrown into a pond—ripples that finally lap against the farther shore.

If that is true of physical reality and of our own spiritual experience, how much more must it be true of Jesus Christ! His being here, all that he was and did, makes a difference in the way things are. This is the world in which he came and lived and loved and suffered and died and rose again and still lives to make himself known to men. It is a world which is like that. So Jesus Christ is not some accidental or incidental event. He is a supremely significant event, with results far beyond anything that we can think or see or hear or know. Above all, because in him God and man were inextricably one, the results will be all the more widespread, all the more decisive, all the more significant.

We must not make Jesus Christ and his whole significance a merely parochial, this-worldly, affair. Christian thought has insisted that in Jesus Christ the Word of God—which is the New

Testament phrase for God in his self-expressive, outward-moving, creative and revelatory action—is present and active in a full and true and genuine Man. If this is the case, then what Jesus does is what God is always up to.

When God does a new thing, nothing can be the same afterward. When God brought life out of inanimate matter, through a gradual process of evolution, things were different. When God brought out of living matter consciousness and self-determination, again through a gradual process of evolution, things were different. And when God united himself to manhood in Jesus Christ, again after a long process in which he indwelt and acted within the human race, things were different. This ought to deliver us from "teeny-weeny" thoughts about Jesus Christ and what he is and does.

So when we accept him and commit ourselves to him, we are not just getting out of the situation in which we find ourselves. We are beginning to live a new kind of life in a new kind of world. We are actually being taken into the life of "God-in-manhood"; and we are being enabled to make actual the truth about ourselves as we are in God's sight. We are new men, complete men, in Christ.

7

WHO IS JESUS CHRIST?

It is now time for us to give a more detailed consideration to the Man of Nazareth who in some remarkable way has become the living Lord of untold millions of people during the past two thousand years and who still continues to hold this position for millions of people in the world today.

Born in Palestine in the distant past, his career lived out in a relatively obscure province of the Roman Empire at that time, his death an ignominious one on a criminal's cross, Jesus has yet become an inescapable factor in human history, with whom thinking men and women of every age must come to terms. His death, as John Masefield makes a character say in his play *The Trial of Jesus*, has "let him loose into the world, where neither Jew nor Greek can stop him."

His teaching, with its emphasis on the reign of God in the affairs of men, still remains, twenty centuries later, the highest known to mankind and, in words once uttered by a Christian thinker, has "become the conscience of the world." He himself, embodying that teaching in his own life, is alive among us as the voice of that conscience; and even those who do not accept Christian belief about him can say, like John Stuart Mill, the Victorian economist and philosopher, that the best possible standard for men's conduct is to live in such a fashion that Jesus of Nazareth would approve of them. Those who disregard what he said and what he was are obliged at least to pay him lip-service. And for millions of men and women throughout the world and for all these centuries, he is Master and Lord.

On any reckoning, he is the most important man who ever lived; and it is entirely appropriate that we should divide history into "B.C.," or "Before Christ," and "A.D.," or the "Year of the Lord" which comes "After Christ." He is the turning-point in human history. His coming, as one of his earliest spokesmen, Paul of Tarsus, put it, was "in the fullness of the times"; and even those who do not profess and call themselves Christians must admit that he has made more difference than anyone else who has lived and spoken in human terms.

With all this in mind, therefore, it is not exaggerating the truth to say that one of the marks of a truly human mind, open to the facts, is its serious attention to Jesus Christ. Who is he? What should be our attitude toward him?

The record of the life of Jesus can be read in those books of the New Testament called the Gospels. These four books or booklets, called after the names of St. Matthew, St. Mark, St. Luke, and St. John, were written at the most seventy-five years after the crucifixion of Jesus. Three of them—Matthew, Mark, and Luke—are much earlier than that; and one of these, Mark, probably dates from the early sixties of the first century, hardly more than thirty years after the events which it records. Experts who have made a careful and scholarly investigation of the sources tell us that much of the material found in Matthew and Luke was set down before that time, perhaps as early as the mid-forties of the first century. And the letters written by Paul of Tarsus as he traveled about the Mediterranean world proclaiming Christ as Lord and asserting that he is the central figure and the saving power in God's relationship with men, were written within fifteen years, in some instances, of Jesus' historical life in Palestine.

Nobody who has taken the time and the trouble to make a

82

thorough study of the facts has the slightest reason to question that the Gospels give us a picture of Jesus which in the main is entirely accurate. Even the modifications which we see from Gospel to Gospel, the occasional "heightening" of the miraculous element in the story to which critics of Christianity have often called attention, are in themselves testimony to the overwhelming power of the impression which the historic life made upon men. There is really no escaping from the fact of the historic Jesus. All we can do is try to understand his significance and make a place for him in our scheme of things.

Born to a peasant mother, the child Jesus grew up in a rural section of his country, living the ordinary life of a Jewish boy of the time, attending the synagogue school, doubtless assisting Joseph, an artisan in the village of Nazareth. In his early manhood he believed himself called by God to a special work. He was to continue, with changes, the work of an earlier prophetic figure, known as John the Baptizer because he had his followers baptized when they had heard his message and accepted its truth. This work was the proclaiming of the Reign of God and the assertion of the demands that Reign makes upon the lives of men. Jesus, like John, declared that the Reign of God was coming, that men must prepare for its coming, and that in the degree to which they were ready and living in terms of the Reign's demands, they would be fit to enter into it when it came.

Because Jesus was a Jew of his own time, he naturally conceived of that Reign ("the Kingdom of God" or "the Kingdom of Heaven") in terms which were familiar to the Jewish people of his day. It was to mark the end of life on the old pattern, the beginning of life with a new pattern. Its coming would have a catastrophic character, for it would introduce into men's experience a new factor—the dreadful, yet merciful, Reality of God directly at work in the affairs of this world.

Life in the Realm of God would be marked by what the New

Testament calls "love." But that love was very different from our own somewhat sentimentalized version of the word: it would be a just and holy love, requiring self-sacrifice, self-giving, a complete dedication and commitment to the goodness of God and an unselfish sharing with all men. Even now, before the Realm came, God demanded that men should live in this way. Only so could they be perfect as their heavenly Father was perfect. And they would be judged, as to whether they were worthy of the Realm when it came, by the quality of their lives, understood in these terms.

Jesus did not only teach, he acted. What he did was in complete agreement with what he said. As he taught that men should live in utter charity one with another under the rule of a just and loving God, so he acted to make God's justice and goodness a potent reality in the affairs of men. He "went about doing good," one of the books of the New Testament says. His invigorating personality drew men and women to him; his kindness and understanding attracted little children. Confronted by sickness, he used the faith which he awakened in others to effect cures for them; yet he declined to become merely a faith-healer to the exclusion of his mission of proclaiming the coming Realm of God.

The records contained in the Gospels tell us of even mightier works, in which the very forces of nature were obedient to him: he is said to have stilled a storm, to have multiplied a few loaves and fishes so that they were sufficient to feed a great multitude, to have walked on the water in his coming to his disciples distressed by a raging sea. Whatever some may think of the nature miracles, as they have been called, and however we may wish to interpret both their happening and their significance, one thing remains absolutely certain. To those who knew him and felt the enormous impact of his personality upon their lives, it was

84

entirely credible that he should have done these things. That in itself is significant testimony to the kind of person he was.

He dared to challenge the authorities of the Jewish people. Content in their claim that they were indeed God's chosen representatives, these authorities had succumbed to the temptations of pride, arrogance, self-seeking, substitution of their own theories for the will of God, which are so often found in persons in places of great power. Rulers asserted themselves rather than the God for whom they were commissioned to speak and act. With utter fearlessness Jesus denounced such men as "blind leaders of the blind." He dared to call them "hypocrites" and people who "played at being good." Naturally, their enmity was aroused, for they saw that Jesus was winning the great masses of the common people, who "heard him gladly" because he spoke simply, compellingly, with a stern affection, yet with utter understanding and complete authority.

As he continued his work, over many months (we do not know the exact number, for the Gospels are somewhat confusing as to the length of what is called Jesus' "public ministry"), he came to see more and more deeply the nature of his own unique vocation. He had proclaimed the coming of God's Realm, he had spoken of the demands which it made upon men, he had wrought good works to help God's human children, and he had boldly denounced hypocrisy and pride.

But that was not all he had to do. He himself was now to act, starkly and challengingly. It was God's will that he should go to Jerusalem, the great and beautiful headquarters of Judaism, there to give the supreme challenge: "God's will must be done; it will be done; those who fail to do it will be rejected or destroyed when the Reign of God comes upon us." What this meant was that Jesus believed that until and unless the whole people, speaking through their responsible leaders, accepted this proclamation and the demands which it involved, they were to be cast out of the coming kingdom; they would have no place in the Realm of God.

He went to the city accompanied by a small band of his chosen friends or disciples. And his challenge was given. Given— and rejected. But Jesus now came to an even deeper understanding of God's will for him and for the work in which he was engaged. Even if he was rejected—we can even say, *because* he was rejected—God would yet accomplish the purpose which he had in view. For through the rejection of Jesus, and the death which Jesus would necessarily suffer as one who had ventured to criticize the people who believed that they were the chosen of God, the Realm of God would in fact be brought in, and a new life of men with God and of God among men would be released into the world.

This was the destiny which was marked out for Jesus. He embraced it with supreme courage and confidence. He followed it unswervingly to the end. He was arrested, tried, condemned, crucified. He was put to death for declaring what he was convinced was God's will and for daring to act upon it.

The extraordinary and deeply moving thing is that as we read the pages of the New Testament which tell this story, and especially as we read the account in the Gospel according to St. Mark—with its direct, unadorned style, in which as the author tells of the trial and death not one single adjective is used to gain effect—we feel that Jesus moves through the whole scene as the central and victorious figure. Here is no passive acceptance of fate; here, rather, is the active accomplishment of a mighty work. An old friend of mine, the austere and unemotional literary critic and philosopher Paul Elmer More, once remarked to me that he could never read that narrative in St. Mark without tears; but that it was not pity for Jesus but awe in the presence of human grandeur that brought the tears to his eyes.

The death on the cross was but the prelude to the really new and astonishing fact with which Christianity, as a matter of simple history, is most concerned. For "this Jesus whom ye crucified, God hath made him both Lord and Christ." "Death hath no more dominion over him." "God raised him from the dead" for "he could not be holden of death." The details of what we call the Resurrection are of slight importance in comparison with the shattering truth that Jesus Christ, who had been killed by the hatred, jealousy, pride, and arrogance of men, triumphed over death on Easter Day. He appeared to the disciples, in a manner beyond our understanding. He appeared to them, they tell us, giving them what they name as "many infallible signs" that he was truly alive, in all the integrity of manhood. And in the strength of that conviction, the disciples went out to preach and to teach that the human master whom they had known and loved and served was the Lord of heaven and earth, through whom God's reign of love had been brought to men, and by whose action every man and woman, in every land and at every time, could enter into newness of life, finding salvation in his name. He was alive, alive from the dead; and he was the abiding companion of those who gave themselves to him and to his cause.

These are the facts about the historic Jesus, as they are reported to us in the Gospels, which tell of what was remembered about him and of what he was believed to have done. Who then can he be?

To this question, so relevant to the experience of the earliest Christian believers and so vital to all who since that day have been exposed to the dynamic personality of Jesus Christ, the greatest thinkers of Christian history and, indeed, of the world since the days when he was with us "in the flesh," have given their whole minds. Their conclusions, accepted with enthusiasm by the company of believers, have come to be embodied in what is called "the dogma of the Incarnation."

Often this word "dogma" troubles modern people. It need not do so, at least in this respect, for it only means the agreed and accepted belief which Christians have found to be necessary if their deepest faith in Jesus Christ is to be maintained and preserved. And the word "Incarnation," which may also cause trouble to some, means only the "en-man-ment" of God—that God has lived in a true human life in the Man Jesus who is our Brother as well as our Lord.

The Apostles' Creed affirms, in its second paragraph, that the Christian believes "in Jesus Christ, his [God's] only Son our Lord: Who was conceived by the Holy Ghost, Born of the Virgin Mary: Suffered under Pontius Pilate, Was crucified, dead, and buried; He descended into hell; The third day he rose again from the dead: He ascended into heaven, And sitteth on the right hand of God the Father Almighty; From thence he shall come to judge the quick and the dead . . ."

That Creed is a brief statement of what the earliest Christians actually proclaimed as they journeyed about the Greco-Roman world preaching the "gospel" or the "good news" about Jesus Christ. This gospel was very simple, yet very profound. Despite a popular misunderstanding, it did *not* consist in saying that "God is our Father and all men should live like brothers." On the contrary, it consisted in the bold declaration that "in Christ God was reconciling the world to himself." Or again, that "while we were yet sinners, Christ died for us." Or again, that "God so loved the world that he gave his only begotten Son, that whoso believeth in him should not perish but have eternal life." In a single phrase, it was the statement that "Jesus is Lord" —and that meant, for men of the time, that he was the present, living, ruling, saving One. In him God had acted to bring men to himself, so that they might once again be truly the men God intended and wished them to be.

Now the Creed puts this proclamation in simple, story form.

88

A recent writer has correctly noted that the Creed asserts that in the great drama of human life, God is the chief actor. Through Christ, he has come as never before on to the stage of human history, in him has lived out a human life, known in that Man Jesus what it means to experience death, has conquered death by his action and has raised from the dead that Man Jesus in "all that pertains to the perfection of human nature."

God has come; and, however we may envisage it, he will come again—in Christ—"to judge the quick and the dead," to crown and complete the work which he has begun. It is told in a story, about One who came and lived and loved and suffered and died and rose again and evermore lives among men and with God; about One who in some fashion which our human minds cannot fathom will vindicate his work by "coming again" to judge all men in terms of their response to his "first coming." Have men lived in *his* way, responded to that for which *he* stood, made *his* will their master-light? or have they gone on their own way, selfishly, proudly, arrogantly, lovelessly, moving with a strange self-determination toward destruction?

That is what the Creed is concerned to say. Admittedly much of the language of this ancient formulation is "pictorial," as we like to put it. Some of the account is in terms that we would not wish to employ, if we were writing the Creed today. Certain of the clauses must be understood, for precise knowledge, by a study of the thought-patterns of the people of an age long since gone. But even as it stands, with all these points allowed, it conveys to us the supreme fact. By Christ, in terms of Christ, through Christ, men are confronted by God, and their whole existence depends upon whether they accept or reject him, once they have really and honestly faced him.

Again, the Creed is the creed of the Christian Church. It can be properly understood only from within the company of Christian believers. It is not a series of hurdles in belief which one must jump before he can qualify as a Christian at all. Those who are outside cannot get inside the Creed until they are inside the Church. And when the Church is doing its proper business, it is seeking by all fair means to get people "inside" so that they can understand and appropriate what the Creed is asserting, and by that understanding and appropriation find the newness of life which God in Christ makes available for them.

It is by the assertions of the Creed concerning Jesus—or, in a better phrasing, by the Jesus concerning whom the Creed speaks —that the Christian Church lives. Without him, it would be nothing but another association or society of men and women and children. Unless he is the Lord and God's special and unique Son among men (which is what the phrase "only Son" means), the Christian Church is a pointless and motley human organization. With him, and with him as Lord and Son of God, the Church is what the New Testament calls it: the "Body of Christ" here in the world, to do what Jesus' physical body did for him in Palestine, which is to make him known, to be the instrument for his work in the world even today, to express his will, and to make him a present and inescapable fact in the experience of men.

We can best get at the meaning of the phrase, "the dogma of the Incarnation," by looking at what Jesus did and does, for it is only because of what he did and does, that we can learn who he was and is. He still continues to bring men and women together with God in a new and wonderful way wherever men turn to him. For example, he brings God near to us, so that we can say that in Jesus the God who seemed so far off, beyond the skies, is now humanly knowable and lovable. He makes God real, vivid, vital, to men and women, rather than remote and uninterested in them and their affairs. He provides men and women with an object of worship which is close at hand.

Above all, he gives grace to men and women—which means

that he brings a power or strength to their lives which enables them to live rightly with God and in love and charity with their fellows. In doing this he wipes away their imperfection and sin, and restores them to a free and open fellowship with God. He brings to them a proportion about things, a perspective on things, and a power to handle things.

All this, and more, is what is described when we speak of the "Atonement" between God and man which was achieved by God in the Man Jesus Christ. After all the word "atonement" breaks down into "at-one-ment"; and it was exactly such an "at-one-ment" between God and men, and in consequence between man and man, which Jesus wrought out in his whole life, and supremely in his death and Resurrection. That is why he is called "the Savior of the world."

Finally, he does that great act of completing man, of fulfilling him, of making him be what he was created to be, which is our supreme need. He is *the* Man, precisely because he is Man united with God, the conjoined organ or instrument for God, who is the supreme and all-fulfilling Reality.

If Jesus Christ has done these things, if he is indeed the Savior of the world and the Consummator of our human nature, he must be One who speaks and acts not only from our side, as Man, but from God's side too. Of course he is truly human, a Man among men. But he must be more than that, for no man can redeem others from their sin, restore them to full fellowship with God, establish in them the completion of their human nature, and "open to them the gate of everlasting life." Only *God* can do that. In some most profound and genuine sense, then, there must be in this human life, this Man, the presence and the working of God. Jesus Christ must be more than this Man; he must be this Man in whom God acts in a decisive, as well as in a supreme manner. It is precisely this which the Christian Church, throughout its long history, has asserted about him.

A great Christian philosopher who was also a humble Christian believer put this assertion in the following words: "A life which is at once everywhere creaturely [that is, human], and yet also everywhere more than creaturely [that is, divine]; because its limitations, circumscriptions, and infirmities, whatever they may be, interpose no obstacle to the divine and eternal purpose which controls and shines through it, but are themselves vehicles of that purpose." A. E. Taylor, who wrote this, went on to say, "That there has been one human life of which this is a true description, and that that is the life of the Founder of Christianity, is the conviction which gives the Christian religion its specific character."

Thus there are three things we ought to say, if we are Christians, when we speak about "who Jesus is." First, that he is genuinely human. Second, that in him there is a true presence and action of God. Third, that he was one fully integrated personality in whom God and man are thus utterly and enduringly united, as intimately and fully as God and man can be united. In his true manhood the presence and action of God are crucially focused and expressed, to the intent that all other men may be caught up into and share that divine-human relationship.

Let us consider in a little more detail what is involved in the three statements about Jesus Christ in the above paragraph.

He is genuinely human. If God is to be known by men and to work among them in a fashion which makes a decisive difference in their lives, he must do this somewhere, at some time, under some particular conditions, and in some given circumstances. Thus Jesus, in whom God was thus present and in action in true human life, was a Jew of the first century of the era which we call after his name. He thought and acted as a man, a Jew of that time. When we say that he was "genuinely human" we must go on to add that he was the perfection of humanity. In him, as we find him portrayed in the Gospels, there was unity and consistency, so different from the confusion and changefulness which we know in ourselves. There was spiritual assurance and certainty about God's nature and his will. There was serenity which came from conformity, by free consent, with the will or purpose of God for him. There was penetrating insight which went straight to the heart of things, cutting through all evasions and duplicity. There was tenacity of purpose which sprang from his clear understanding of what his work was to be. For every one of these statements, ample evidence may be adduced from the stories of his historical life in Palestine.

If we want to know what human life really is, as God plans it and wills it, there is one place to look: Jesus Christ. He is all that we could wish to be, all that we know we ought to be—although naturally he is *that* in his own historical circumstances so that he cannot just be copied as an artist reproducing a masterpiece would try exactly to copy the original. The way we "imitate" Christ is by letting ourselves be caught by his Spirit, filled with his influence, molded by his insight and personality. Yet the consistency, certainty, serenity, insight, and tenacity which he had are what human life ought always to manifest. As we read the story of his human life, we come to see that Christ is truly man, in the complete and adequate sense of the word.

Again, there is in him a true presence and action of God. Some people, who count themselves very orthodox, will doubtless object to the way in which I have phrased it. But they will agree that the statement is true, so far as it goes. And they will agree further that to speak, as Christians do, of the "divinity of Christ" does not mean that he is to be regarded as the best man who ever lived, although that surely is true too. To say only that, however, would be to regard him as the finest of human achievements. Yet people who have been confronted by what he has done and what he is, do not feel inclined to applaud him as a great human achievement. They are impelled, like Charles Lamb, the essayist, in a story told by his friend William Hazlitt, to wish "to fall on their knees and kiss the hem of his garment." He comes to us as a divine arrival, a gift to men, although that gift is given to us in the human terms that we can appreciate and understand.

The God who created the whole world and everything in it, who works ceaselessly in nature and history, who is revealed in the beauty, the courage, the goodness, the love, which men recognize and revere—this God, Christians believe, has done something more and something supremely more important. He has "taken our nature upon him," as the prayer for the Christmas celebration of the Holy Communion puts it—that is, he has united to himself a human life which he has made his own. He has done this not by violating or outraging humanity, but by being present and active in One of our own kind. It is in Jesus Christ that he has done this; and he has done it there in a fashion nowhere else known, with an intensity nowhere else even imagined, in a degree that is immeasurably different from his other presences and his other actions.

As our third statement makes clear, he has done this in one fully integrated personality in whom God and man are indeed utterly and enduringly united. Nothing that properly belongs to human nature is absent, for Jesus Christ is human in body, mind, and soul or spirit. But God has himself become the "divine and eternal purpose" which controls and shines through the whole life of the Man born of Mary. God and man are at one in him. They are at one in a personality that is not split, divided, "mixed-up" or "messed-up." They are one in a human being who is manhood at its completest—because manhood, when it is complete, is manhood which is used by God as it freely and gladly responds to his presence and his action.

If I employ my right hand to represent God and my left hand

to represent man, I can bring them together and clasp them in a loose fashion, breaking the clasp now and again, perhaps most of the time only touching them one to the other. That is the way it is with God and the rest of us. But I can also bring them together so tightly that they become, as it were, one thing. In Jesus, God and man are brought into this unity; they make *one thing*. They are so at one that they can never be broken apart. Thus in everything that Jesus does and says as a man, God is working and acting, God is present, God is speaking and looking at men and bringing them to himself.

That is the answer to the question, "Who is Jesus Christ?"

8

WHAT DO CHRISTIANS BELIEVE?

(Part I)

Some people would say that Christianity is a set of ideals which ought to be followed. Others would suggest that it is a collection of ideas about God and man. Still others would urge that it is a collection of beliefs. There are many who would describe it in terms of worship and prayer. There are even some who think that it means nothing more than the admittedly important business of being decent and fair to one's fellow-men and in this fashion promoting more good will and mutual understanding in the world.

But Christianity is much bigger, much richer, and much more concrete than any one of these definitions or than all of them put together. It is a complex unity in which living, worshiping, and believing people are knit together by their great conviction that in the Man Christ Jesus God has united himself supremely with humanity; and that they are enabled to share in the life of God through the fellowship which came into existence with the coming of Jesus Christ into the world.

That is where we must begin when we think about what Christians believe. But we ought now to be able to go on and speak more specifically of the content of the Christian belief, for it is Christian belief which determines the specific character of Christian worship and the specific way of life which is properly called by the Christian name. So first, about GOD.

God, G-O-D, is only a little three-letter word, and a word which we tend to use too glibly. Much better perhaps, if we followed Matthew Arnold's suggestion and kept the word "God" for the great occasions. The wealth of its meaning, the sweep which it includes, the richness of its implications for prayer and worship—all these should make us say "God" with hesitation and with awe. For who is God?

He is not just a religious idea, as so many people seem to think —like the lady who told her pastor that it was blasphemous for him even to hint that God could exist apart from our belief in him! He is not just something said in Church, or someone thought about only there. On the contrary, he is the one enduring, dependable, eternally sure Reality, who is in and behind and through every single thing that has ever happened, ever does happen, or ever will happen. He is the utterly supreme, utterly holy, utterly good, utterly wise Reality, without whom there would be nothing else at all. He is the altogether lovely, unspeakably sublime, everlasting Reality, whose beauty is but palely reflected in all harmony, all music, all earthly glory.

God, then, is the Reality to whom the tiny human word points. But he is more than that. For by God the Christian means something beyond this inescapable Reality, this supreme Truth, this ineffable Beauty. He is the *living* God.

He is the One who has a purpose, a plan, a design, which he is working out in the world that he has created and that he continues day by day to create. He has schemes which are to be accomplished here and now; he made the world with a purpose and he sustains and guides, and everlasting creates anew, so that his purpose may be realized. He calls men to take their place in that design or plan. It will be fulfilled even though we fail our part, for God does not depend on us although he uses us, if we freely consent, to further his ends. He adapts the working of his scheme to the response men make to him, and he allows men to assist him in that scheme; we can be his fellow-workers, open to his influence and thus enabled to be his agents in bringing about some greater goodness, some finer truth, some more glorious beauty, some wider stretch of love in the created order of things. He has so arranged the world that in this co-operation we can find our destiny fulfilled, our human lives completed, and our whole being irradiated with God's very life as we are employed in his service.

Furthermore, God is the One who in surprising and humble self-giving lets us know him. He does not stand aloof and remote from his world or from the men who inhabit it. He comes close to it; or even better put, he dwells in it and it dwells in him--he is *in* everything and everything is *in* him. This, of course, is not a spatial sort of *in* but a presence and an action which are after a spiritual, penetrative manner. Thus he lets us know him not only as the One who is here, but as One whom we can know as we know one another, in what we call personal terms. God, whom (as the Bible says) "heaven, and the heaven of heavens, cannot contain," is the God who dwells with us men, in our secret heart, letting us have fellowship, friendship, comradeship with him, if we will but open ourselves to his presence and his action.

God: a three-letter word; and yet a word which can mean more than any other word in our language, if when we take it on our lips we stop to think, so that we may know whereof we speak. And it is *men* who use it. But, then, what about MAN?

Some people would say that a man is so much of this or that chemical, altogether amounting to a dollar or so's worth of common stuff. And that is true, so far as it goes. Others would say that he is a peculiar complex of instincts, desires, impulses, urges, which drive him on and which may or may not be controlled in some purpose or by some aim. That also is true, so far as it goes. Still others regard man as a social animal, having meaning in his relationships with others in family, state, society. That, too, is true so far as it goes.

None of these definitions is the whole truth about man. The fact is that man is an embodied spirit; he is soul-body or body-soul; he is, to use a phrase of Sir Thomas Browne in *Religio Medici,* an "amphibian" compounded of body and mind, stuff and soul, matter and purpose. He is not these things on various levels, as it were; he is all these things in one whole which is either more and more on the way to perfect integration or more and more on the way to destructive fissure. Man's glory is that he can express himself in this *whole* way; his shame is that he can express himself in such a fashion that he descends to the level of sheer animality—but animality with a difference, for with him it is always a violation of his person to do this and he can never be just like an animal; he can only be a degraded human personality.

Thus man is different from sticks, stones, flowers, and dogs. For not only has he life; he is, in the phrase used in Genesis in the Old Testament, "a living soul." That is, he is personality-in-the-making.

Man is on his way to becoming a self-determining creature. That is his intended destiny. It is this for which God made him and it is toward this that God would have him strive and grow. Alas, unlike sticks, stones, flowers, and dogs, man with his power to choose—to say "yes" or "no" when choices of action are open to him, and to govern his behavior and thought and speech accordingly—has chosen to deny his destiny and to substitute for the freedom of self-determination and self-control the tyranny of chaotic license or that kind of unrestrained activity which follows upon the "liberty which says 'blah.'" Thus man has put himself out of the order of things; he is *inordinate*—he does not live according to plan. So it happens that he is a sinner.

In some of the Christian orders of worship it is directed that those present shall confess themselves to be "miserable sinners." Many dislike this phrase, but in fact it is a very complimentary thing for a man to say. It penetrates to the depths of our human situation. It is complimentary because it says that as sinners we are not what we were meant to be and in God's intention and by his power could be; and because it also says that we are miserable—that is, unhappy, about this sad fact.

But as we saw in an earlier chapter, we are not alone in our sin any more than we are alone in our humanity. We are "social animals," as Aristotle put it. For better or for worse we belong with and we are inalienably associated with our human brethren. In fact, if one were to draw up a complete description of what it means to be a man, he would be obliged to include this social belonging which is an indelible part of our human nature. We are biological creatures, of course; it is not so often recognized that we are social creatures. Any man apart from his fellow-men is to that degree less than human. By this I do not mean that we must be with them in the sense of physical propinquity. That may or may not be the case. But we must be with them in the deeper sense that we belong together with them; that we are influenced by them; that we share together a common sociology; and that man entirely alone, as an individual without relationships with others of his own kind, is not man in any recognizable meaning that the word should possess.

Furthermore, we cannot realize ourselves and come to the completion of our humanity in what used to be described as "splendid isolation." We require—we simply must have—our fellow-men if we are to be what we were meant to be. At what is sometimes called "the natural level" we know this to be true; that is why the family is the normal way in which men live. It is equally true in our religious life—in our relationship with God.

Thus the true picture of man, as Christianity understands it, is a picture which sees him as one of God's children, intended to be a free, self-determined being who lives in association with others, and who with them and in association with their striving moves toward the completion of his personality in relationship to God who made him and wants him to live richly and fully in this world and in whatever future existence may be open to him. But the true picture also includes, as Christianity sees it, the evident fact that man is a sinner, twisted in his living, distorting the image of God in which he is made, inordinate, needing to be set right. And when man is most himself, knows himself most truly and understands his present situation and condition, he cries out, with St. Paul, "O wretched man that I am, who will deliver me?"

To man in his need, God acts in his deed. To man the sinner, caught in his wrong use of divinely given powers, and unable to extricate himself from the involvement which frustrates his true humanity, the supremely holy and altogether lovely Reality whom we call God comes in mercy and compassion.

He does not send a message, merely; nor does he announce, as if from on high, his forgiveness. He does not pronounce words. Rather, he *comes*. Of course that word should not be understood in the spatial sense, as if God moves from one place to another. He need not do that, for he is always here. This is his world; he ceaselessly energizes in it; if he left it, the world would fall apart and dissolve into nothingness. Yet he does come. For in the life of Jesus Christ, bone of our bone and flesh of our flesh, our Brother Man, God "tabernacles." He dwells in this temple which is human flesh and blood, body and soul, mind and spirit. In our common human idiom, he takes up his abode; he lives and moves and has his being. God is made manifest in man, yes, but even more: God is present and active in *this* Man, for us men and for our wholesome, abundant, sound, and healthy living as sons of God, who thus come to our completion and fulfillment, and in this way realize all that God has put it in us to be.

Not that Jesus Christ is God's only entrance into our human world. In fact he does not so much enter it (for that would suggest that otherwise he was absent from it—which would not be Christianity at all) as he expresses or acts in it. And he does this in all sorts of ways and in all degrees of intensity.

Friedrich von Hügel liked to say that Jesus Christ "crowns" what he called God's many "entrances, preveniences, and condescensions to men." By this he meant that God has indeed always been with men, the root and ground of their being, the hidden source of their goodness, the beauty behind all visible things which we style beautiful, the truth which ever urges men on to seek for more truth, the love which shines through all human loving. But never before had God been with men as he was with them in Jesus Christ; never before had he so intimately and enduringly united to himself true human life.

The wonder of it is that it was all so human, even while it was also so utterly divine. For our greater consternation and dread, God might have thundered from the heavens; for our greater loving, and hence for our richer living, he chose to come to us, to unite himself with us, in a tiny baby, held in his Mother's arms. He chose to live in a Man who was one of us, among other men; and never did man speak or live or act as did this Man in whom God dwelt among us. For all the time it was God-in-Man; in every aspect of his life, at every moment of his human experience, on every occasion and in every situation, it was God-in-Man. So as we see him, hear him, walk with him, let his love bind us to him, it is not the humanity alone which is ours. It is very God of very God, present and active in that humanity; it is the God who ever creates the universe, who makes himself felt and known in our own human terms. It is "through the wounds of the most holy humanity," as a French mystic put it, "that we come to the precious intimacy of the divinity"; it is through that same humanity that God has willed to come to us.

This, said Alice Meynell in a beautiful poem, is "the terrible, frightened, whispered, sweet, heart-shattering secret of his way with us." This is the humility of God. This is the salvation, the making-whole and the making-complete, of our manhood. God dwells with us in this human life, where we are. He unites us to himself as we respond in love and loyalty to Jesus Christ his Son our Lord. He does what an old Christian, St. Irenaeus, once described in surprising words: "He becomes altogether what we are, that he might make us altogether what he is."

Our response, then, is very simple, however searching and difficult. We are to kneel before him as one receiving a divine gift, given in terms which we can understand and appropriate. Then, in the power of that gift, we are to go out, with him as our Master and Savior and Lord, reconciled to God, put right again as his children; we are to go out into the common ways of life, letting him shine through our lives so that other man may through us be loved back into God's plan.

It is at this point that we can begin to see the meaning of THE CHURCH.

When Jesus Christ ended the days of his flesh in Palestine, he left behind him in the world of time and space and historical existence—what?

Some have thought that what was left behind was a new view of God and man and their relationship. Others have said it was a new idea about the meaning of human life. Still others have thought it was a set of ethical principles which should govern men's behavior. And there have been some who felt that a series of dogmas called "the Catholic faith" was left behind. In fact, it was none of these, although all of these have come into being through that which he did truly leave behind him. What he left behind was himself. Himself, that is all. But he left himself as being made available to men through a new society, a new fellowship, what the Anglican Prayer Book calls "the blessed company of all faithful people"—which is to say the Church of Christ. Jesus had dwelt with men, and through that dwelling had brought God nearer than he had ever before been known to be in human experience. Now he continued to dwell with men, risen from the dead and known to men in the community of the Church which became what St. Paul called "the body of Christ."

In that fellowship, Jesus Christ is risen to be with his people and with all men if they will commit themselves to him. He is brought near. He continues to do his work of loving men back into God's plan and redeeming their broken and frustrated and incomplete lives from futility and triviality into nobility and meaning and completeness.

This is why the Church has been called a "sacred and wonderful mystery." It is not simply an association of men and women who happen to hold some of the same beliefs, who like to worship and pray more or less in the same way, and who accept certain common standards of human behavior. It is "the mystical body of Christ"; the continental Christian thinkers of our own time call it the *Una Sancta*—the one holy fellowship.

Here we are concerned with what Christians have themselves believed about the Church as they have accepted it, lived in it, and worked as its members down through the centuries. First of all, they have said that it is *Christ's* Church, not ours, with our separations and divisions. Since it is his Church, it is *one* Church, even if its manifestation in the world has been a broken one, with the denominational groups which have seemed to split it up and damage its unified witness and life.

One of the important religious movements of our time, known as the "ecumenical movement," has taken these divisions, splittings, groupings very much to heart; and seeing that these damage the unified witness and life of the Church of Christ, that movement is working patiently and faithfully to restore to the Church the visible unity which surely is according to Christ's will. Already much has been accomplished in this direction, and the future looks bright for the eventual re-establishment of one Church visible to men, even as Christians all belong in a deeper sense to the one Church which exists in an unseen manner because it is Christ's Church and he is one Christ.

In the second place, the Church is holy. We have seen that continental Christians like to speak of the *Una Sancta* or one holy fellowship of Christian people. But again, the holiness of the Church does not derive from any virtues possessed by its members; it derives from the holiness of Christ. And that holiness means that in the depths of its existence the Church like its Lord is with God and for God, separated out from all that is not God so that it can bring all that is not God into a relationship with him through sanctifying or making holy the common pursuits and the ordinary experiences of men and women everywhere.

And again, in the third place, the Church is catholic because it is Christ's Church. The word "catholic" is taken from a Greek term which means essentially integrated or whole; so the Church is the body of Christ with the wholeness and integration which come from complete dedication to and union with its Lord. But the word "catholic" has also come to mean universal or for all people; and so, like Christ himself, it is for all men everywhere, making available through its life and its gospel and its worship the One who is able to save to the uttermost those who believe on him.

Finally, and in the fourth place, the Church is apostolic—which again is derived from a Greek word whose meaning is "sent" or "given a mission." The Church is Christ's Church, and as he was sent from the Father to come into the world, so the Church is sent by Christ to continue his work, to make his presence known and to impart his empowering help to those who will accept it. Again, as apostolic, the Church is continuous today with its past history and its development through two thousand years of Christian history. It comes from Christ himself, it is centered in Christ himself and its mission is to bring Christ himself into contemporary experience, thus continuing the work of the first Christian apostles and sharing in the fellowship of which they were the earliest members.

The Church is all these things, Christians believe, because it is Christ's Church and not merely a human society with human aims and objectives. There can be no Church without Jesus Christ. And nobody can really know and accept Jesus Christ apart from the Church. For even if there are those who are not "of the Church" but yet know and love the Lord Jesus, it has been through the Church and because of the Church's faith that they have come to know him and love him. A contemporary scholar, John Knox, has put it thus: "The Church is the community which remembers Jesus." But Professor Knox has gone on to say that the Church is also the community which is instinct with his Spirit. As such, it has carried through the ages the memory of Jesus in the days when he walked in Palestine, while at the same time it has been enabled to impart his Spirit, his presence and his power, to succeeding ages. Thus when a modern non-churchman speaks of Jesus Christ, his knowledge of him and whatever touch of his Spirit may pervade his life is really a gift which he has received, often quite unconsciously, from the Church itself. For the Church does not "remember" Jesus in pious reverie, looking back over two thousand years to the days under the Syrian sky; it remembers him by bringing him into the present, by making him to be present still, in our contemporary world.

All of this is true, in spite of the sin, the error, and the weakness of those who belong to the Church and of the Church itself in what might be called its empirical manifestation—its obvious visible, organizational form as we see it and know it in our various denominations and sects. Most wonderful and surprising of all the wonders and surprises in God's way with his human children, is the fact that in and through this strange, ill-assorted, mixed bag, this visible band of men and women who call themselves Christian, God in Christ still works in the world.

That God should deign to use what St. Augustine called this *corpus permixtum*—this strangely assorted collection of people who constitute the Church—is an occasion for human gratitude and rejoicing. It is also an occasion for our penitence, since Christian people are not worthy of such use by God. It is a call to resolve and determination that the visible Church, here in this world as men see it and know it, shall by God's grace and our determined and resolved action, become more perfectly that which in God's intention and in its deepest reality it already is— the place where wayfaring men and women have their meeting with Christ and through him with the God who dwells in him. The Church is the body of Christ; and it is every day to become more and more what it really is.

But how does the Church accomplish its mission? The answer to this question may be found in looking once again at the three characteristics which mark all religious groups—belief or creed, worship and prayer or cult, and conduct and discipline or life. Thus the Church has a three-fold task and it applies itself to fulfilling that task.

First of all, it preaches the gospel. It proclaims the good news that in Christ God was present and active; that there men are reconciled to God and thus become complete men, restored to their true nature as men. When it has done this, it must go on to think about the message it proclaims. Therefore it works out a set of beliefs, whose importance is not in their value as human speculation but in their capacity to maintain and preserve the gospel which the Church is commissioned to preach.

In the second place, the Church offers worship to God as he has made himself known in Christ. This finds its chief expression in the sacraments which are part of the Church's heritage. The Church also guides and assists men in their personal dedication to God, through its teaching and its encouraging its people to engage in prayer.

Finally, there is Christian "action." This means both the day-by-day effort on the part of the Christian disciple to reflect in his life something of the Spirit of Jesus Christ, and also his concern that others shall be brought to share in the same experience and thus become his fellow-disciples. The missionary work of the Church is included under the latter concern of the Christian. In lands already more or less Christian, as well as in parts of the earth where the name of Christ is not known or accepted, the Church labors to bring men and women to the knowledge of him and faith in him. It does this, not by telling others that they are bound to be damned unless they accept, or by saying that until they have thus heard and accepted they have been completely without any knowledge of God, but rather by seeking to share with others, wherever and whoever they may be, the experience which already means so much to those who have met Christ and been grasped by his compelling person and his loving work for men. In that sharing, Christians believe, all the partial light and grace which men everywhere have known from the God who always moves in upon and works within his children, will be brought to a glorious fulfillment and completion, even as those who accept him as Lord will themselves also be brought to such fulfillment and completion.

9

WHAT DO CHRISTIANS BELIEVE?

(PART II)

THERE is an old saying that only two things are certain: "death and taxes." Nobody nowadays would question the certainty of taxes, but it is a strange fact that very few of us are prepared to face up to the reality of death. And yet we know that each one of us will be a corpse, whether in the near future or after some years. A New York surgeon once remarked to a group of students to whom he was lecturing on the progress of medical science: "But do not forget, gentlemen, that with all this advance, the mortality rate remains at one hundred per cent."

Frequently novelists and others have put the blame for this modern refusal to contemplate the fact of death at the door of the undertakers. It is much more likely that it is the other way round. The undertaker is simply reflecting in his practice of so preparing a body for burial that death is made as inoffensive as possible, the prevalent unwillingness to reckon with the stark reality. This is all the more surprising when we remember how many men and women have been killed in recent years through wars which should have brought the fact of death home to us all. Any clergyman, for example, can testify that one reason why death comes, as it often does, as a frightful shock to the survivors is that they have never included death in their picture of human existence. Hence they are not prepared for it when it comes suddenly to one whom they know and love.

But whether we like it or not, accept it or not, death is a fact. And it is a fact with which the Christian Church has always reckoned. Yet even here there is often misunderstanding. Many Christian people, and unhappily some Christian ministers too, have thought that the Christian way of reckoning with death is to deny its reality by emphasizing immortality, or the future life, in such a way that death itself becomes a mere incident with little significance. An old friend of mine used to tell of a pastor whose custom it was, when visiting a home immediately after a death, to enter the house and say, loudly and clearly, "There is no death." My friend commented, "That was a damnable lie, for the body was often still in the house."

The Christian attitude toward death neither minimizes its importance nor denies its reality. The Christian attitude is, first, an honest recognition of the fact, with no attempt to deny its terrible actuality; and second, a faith which sees through death to the God who can and does make death his servant.

The fact of death means the finality of life. That is to say, death puts an end to this mortal existence. We have a limited time to live as mortal men in this present world. A few years added to this period, thanks to the valuable and praiseworthy advance of medical science, cannot change the plain truth that nobody lives, as a mortal in this present world, forever. We may ridicule our ancestors who often said that they wished to "prepare for death," but it remains true that every man or woman who honestly seeks to look facts straight in the face ought to include in his thinking about his own existence the *finis* which death sooner or later will put to that existence. Seeing that this is so, he ought to live as one who knows that he is going to die.

When I say this, I am not suggesting anything unnecessarily morbid. It would be silly to expect people, who are busy about many things and who are enjoying so far as they can their days in this world, to spend all their time brooding on their future death. There is too much to do in this world for such an attitude to be practical or healthy. But it is equally absurd to forget the fact of death altogether. What is possible and what is, for the Christian, necessary is that one should have as a kind of awareness in the depths of one's being the frank recognition that we are mortal men.

Not only does this make it clear to us that we should not lose our sense of proportion about life—for, after all, "you can't take it with you"—and by this honest recognition come to see that it is idiotic to put all our human trust in things which we can accumulate here and now. It also makes clear to us that the wise man understands his own expendability in this world.

Thus we can be delivered from that subtle kind of pride which assumes that everything depends upon us. If we are Christians we can understand that while God does indeed use us for the working out of his purpose, he does not suffer total defeat when our small contribution can no longer be made.

This sane point of view does not lead to moral irresponsibility: "Let us eat and drink, for tomorrow we die." On the contrary, it makes our attitude toward our own existence genuinely Christian, in that like Jesus Christ we gladly and freely commend ourselves and our work to our Creator, knowing that if we thus commend ourselves and our work we can trust, with an invincible Christian conviction, that God will use whatever we are and whatever we do in the accomplishment of his own good purposes. So we are delivered from "faithless fears and worldly anxieties."

The contemporary German existentialist thinker, Martin Heidegger, has taken as one of the ground-truths of his philosophy this recognition of the fact of our human mortality. For him there is a positive as well as a negative side to death. Not only does our death demonstrate the finality of our mortal existence; it also makes clear that we, who know that we die, are beings of a peculiar kind in this great world. If death is the finality of life, it is also life in its finality. As those who are going to die, we live with zest, since we shall not pass this way again. Thus every experience, every relationship, every piece of work, has the kind of interest and gives us the kind of joy which comes when we know that this is something we have but for a time. Hence we can have both delight in and detachment from it. "The world passeth away, and the desires thereof"—therefore (not in spite of the fact) we go through life as pilgrims, finding a tang in our work and in our very existence which is denied to those who are too well settled in the land.

The Christian attitude to death includes not only the honest facing of the fact, with its recognition of our mortality and the consequent zest which attaches to our existence here as pilgrims and wayfarers. It also includes a faith which sees through death to God, who is the lord of death as well as of life. That is why Christian thinking has always centered, not as some have believed in natural immortality, but in resurrection from the dead.

Immortality usually means that there is some part of man, called his soul, which never dies but which because of its own immortal nature will ever go on. This is essentially an idea derived from the ancient Greek philosophers like Socrates. Something like it may or may not be true, although it is hard to see how assurance of a mere prolongation of existence or a future life as a disembodied soul could provide much occasion for joy. In any event, the Christian way of looking at the matter is in terms of resurrection, not of immortality.

Here a great many moderns have a real difficulty. For them the concept of resurrection has been taken to mean—thanks to the bad teaching which they have received, or perhaps because of some overly literal interpretation of pictorial language—that our present physical body, with its chemicals, will somehow be reconstituted and rise from the grave. It is a tragedy that this confusion has arisen, because it is not found in the great source of resurrection teaching—the fifteenth chapter of St. Paul's First Epistle to the Corinthians. There we are told that "God giveth it a body as it pleaseth him," that "flesh and blood cannot inherit the kingdom of heaven," and that the "body of the resurrection," far from being a "physical body," is in St. Paul's own phrase a "spiritual body."

Of course the only way we who live in this world of physics and chemistry can picture a "spiritual body" is through our experience of what it means to have such a body as we now possess. We cannot jump out of our skins, so to say; and our understanding is limited to the sort of pictures which we can form, through our imagination, of a body which will serve beyond the grave the purposes which in this present world our physical bodies serve. None the less, we should be very careful not to confuse the pictures which we necessarily employ with the reality to which those pictures are intended to point. Chemistry and physics do not belong, as such, to the kingdom of heaven.

What the picture of the resurrection of the body is meant to affirm is something like this. Beyond and through death, the God who created life in the first instance and continues to create it in every succeeding instance, re-creates life out of death; he takes our present embodied personalities and remakes them after the pattern of his Son Jesus Christ, whose death and resurrection are therefore types of our own. "Christ the first fruits . . . afterward, them that are Christ's"—and this tells us that after Christ's pattern and in the power which is his by his rising-again from death, God will give us the perfect fruition of our personality in the "spiritual body" which God will create afresh out of the death of our mortal body.

Now all this depends, not upon the deliverance of wise philosophers or the cogent reasoning of great thinkers, neither upon the discoveries which may be made in the realm of psychical research. It is based upon one thing and one thing only: faith in God himself. That faith includes the fact which is also known through faith, that as God raised Jesus Christ from death, so also he will "quicken" us. The Christian, then, has what an old prayer calls "a religious hope," not a philosophical surmise or a scientific demonstration. God is and God will do. That is the logic of faith.

If the Christian belief be such as we have said, then the fact of our mortality will be seen in a quite different light from that which an unbeliever might be able to perceive. For those who have committed themselves to God in Christ, life even now is lived "in Christ." We already have what might be called "a stake in the heavenly kingdom." This is why Christians have so often spoken of this world as a place of "pilgrimage." For that is what it is—a way in which we move toward the native land which is our destiny. That does not for a moment imply that this world is unimportant. How could it be, since God himself has created it, works in it, expresses himself and his purpose through it, and in Jesus Christ united himself with men who live in it? Our task, like that of all true colonists, is to conform this world so far as we can to the vision of the homeland. Thus we are called upon, as Christians, to labor unceasingly to make the charity and the righteousness of God prevail here and now, never resting until they have spread to earth's remotest bounds. Of course, this world, limited as it is in possibilities, can never contain the fullness of God's kingdom. Yet we must also affirm that it can manifest more and more of that kingdom.

The Christian then lives as one who must die, in the steady confidence that God will take care of him and his. He lives also as one who must work in this world to make all things fair, even now. In the end, however, it is not we who do this. All is under God, all is from God, save only our sin and selfishness and pride. "Every virtue we possess, and every victory won . . . are his [God's] alone." Nor does this mean that we are robots, without freedom. On the contrary, our true freedom consists precisely in the service of God, "whose service is perfect freedom."

Here we have a great mystery, but it is not different in kind from the mystery which attaches to all human relationships. It is when we are most dedicated to the service of a person we love or a cause we value, that we feel most free. The man who thinks that he can do what he wants, as he wants it and when he wants it, is the man who is most a prisoner. The man who commits himself to one he loves or to a cause he values has found liberty. And the man who commits himself to God is released from all bondage; in God's will, as Dante said, is man's peace.

For the first time, man can become himself, as God means him to be; he knows "the perfect liberty of the children of God."

Nothing now can "separate him from the love of God in Christ Jesus our Lord," for he has been delivered from the fear that death is the absolute end, as he has also been freed from the illusion that death lacks a final quality, so far as this mortal world is concerned. Above all, he is liberated into that certainty that "God has prepared for them that love him such good things as pass man's understanding," that certainty which gives to human existence its dignity and its glory.

But beyond death . . . what then?

For man, the Christian Church has declared, there are two possible destinies. One is life in God which is eternal and in-destructible; the other is life in self which is disintegrating and miserable. The first would be heaven, the second would be hell. And faith, which takes man seriously and God even more seri-ously, and which would guarantee the moral responsibility of every man, must speak of both of these.

To grow in love toward men as one grows in love toward God —this is man's true path. This is the way to fulfillment and completion. He begins here, in this present world, not to extricate himself from the world with its fleshly mundane realities, but so to live in this world that using it aright he may come to fullness of personality and approach ever nearer to the source of his being who is God. Alone, unaided, he could not do this; inevitably he would stumble and fall. Indeed he does stumble and fall; but he knows also the hand of grace, which stoops to his weakness and lends him the assistance of an almighty love, so that by God's accommodation to our littleness we may share in his greatness.

Man's truest glory, and his greatest cause for rejoicing, is to let himself serve and be served by the omnipotent love of God, which fences him about and seeks in subtle ways to use him for great things. And when his days in this world came to an end, and he has gone as far as he may in what John Keats called this "vale of soul-making," he can then know that God will lovingly purge him of whatever is still false in him, and that after growth and further strengthening he will welcome him to "the company of saints," there to know as he is known in the radiant vision of the altogether lovely One whom we name God.

But man may choose otherwise. He may reject the solicitations of the divine Charity; he may willfully elect to follow his own way, content to live his own life, desirous of nothing but himself and his own little goals. He may seek, in his silly pride, to be an isolated and insulated creature, with no outlet in love or action toward others and toward the God who "made him for himself." Like a stagnant pool, with no way for the water to find a means of outgoing, he soon becomes a stinking horror. And the end of these things? A life alienated from God, not because God willed it or wanted it, but because the man chose it freely—a life without God, hence a life without hope, and hence a disintegrating, self-destroying, miserable life. That is a possible destiny for man. And that would be hell.

Is anybody in that sad case? No one knows. The Church has never said. Not even Judas Iscariot can confidently be placed there. Perhaps nobody comes to that dreadful end. But at least I must never lose sight of the chance that I may be on my way in that direction. That is the awful fact about it. Knowing myself as I do; knowing my rejection of God's various and subtle ways of seeking to win me; knowing my pride, my selfishness, my lovelessness; knowing these things, I must ever pray, "God be merciful to me a sinner." God will be merciful, surely; I can trust him. But I cannot trust in myself. So I must always lean back upon his forgiveness, in the hope and prayer that he will thrust in his sharp sword, shatter my stout resistance, break down my self-seeking, and by so doing, "batter my heart," as John Donne put it, until it becomes by my own grateful response his own.

There is so much more that needs to be said, if one hopes to give a full picture of the belief of the Christian, that the writer despairs of fulfilling his task. But there is at least this one thing more which must be said: it is what the Christian Church affirms about THE HOLY SPIRIT and THE TRIUNE GOD.

Who is the Holy Spirit?

We have already said much about God's ways of working in the world. We have seen that he is ceaselessly active in it, not sitting aloof but ever energizing through the creation. And there have been two sets of statements which have been included, although this may not always have been obvious to the casual reader.

One has had to do with God's self-expressive activity. The other has had to do with his bringing about a response to that self-expression. In the working-out of God's purpose, there has been his "alongsideness" and there has been his action to unite in one thing that "being with his world," and the world's accepting and assimilating and realizing what was going on. From this abstract phrasing, we can approach the meaning of the Holy Spirit.

For the Holy Spirit, in Christian thought, is always that operation of God in his world which is, so to say, "from within." It is the great "Amen" which is said through the creation to God's moving in upon his creation and putting himself alongside it to accomplish his aims. The Holy Spirit is he who, in the depths of the world and in the secret places of historical event, as well as in the profundity of every man's experience, labors to conform nature and history and men to the divine purpose.

"Every virtue we possess, and every victory won . . . are his [God's] alone." The "he" here is, for Christian thought, the Holy Spirit, as the hymn from which the phrase is quoted makes clear. When men respond to God in Christ, when they seek to do his will, when they surrender their lives to his working, when they open their hearts to his influence, when they give themselves to be his servants—when they do this, it is of course *they* who are doing it. But in and through, with and under, *their* doing, there is something else. There is a subtle but real movement of God within them which persuades, urges, suggests, impels. Men in that situation feel that while they are acting in complete freedom, they are also acting under some gentle yet insistent compulsion. This is why they so often will say, not that "they grasped," but that they "were grasped." There is nothing eerie or ghostly about this, for it is the same kind of experience as men have when they find themselves driven or persuaded to embrace a great cause or give themselves to another person in faithfulness and love.

The Christian Church is the community where this kind of

response has been most surely felt. As the first disciples and, later on, those who accepted Jesus as Lord through their preaching and teaching, dedicated their lives in service and worship, in love and obedience, they did not think that this was something which was done all on their own.. It was what somebody has described as "the divine compulsion" which was at work. Furthermore, as that dedication led to a release of energy, a sense of new freedom, an awareness of enhanced life—and you have only to read the Acts of the Apostles and the Epistles in the New Testament to see these things—they were sure that all this came about not so much through their own efforts, although those were needed, as through a working of God within them. This working did not serve as a substitute for any of their normal human capacities and powers; it was not a supplanting of humanity but a presence and a power through the very conditions of human existence.

In an even wider sense, the Christian Church has been prepared to say that wherever men respond in any way to the working of God "upon" them or "alongside" them, there is this presence and power which brings it about. In the world of nature too, there is some capacity, mysterious and wonderful, which leads the inanimate and the animate creation to be what it is meant to be.

D. H. Lawrence once said that it was not he who wrote his poems, "but the wind that bloweth through me." Of course, Lawrence did write his poems, but he had the sense of inspiration (and that means, in exact significance, the Spirit at work in him) which was much more real than his own efforts. Lawrence probably was not thinking of the Holy Spirit; and the fact that he was not so thinking gives all the more weight to his testimony. For the Spirit works everywhere, subtly and compellingly, anonymously and hiddenly. And not only in strictly religious channels, but in all instances where men produce that which is true and good and lovely, or labor for that which is just and righteous, or give themselves to that which is deserving in whatever degree of their loyalty and allegiance.

And this is above all true when men are led to surrender their lives to the God who is present and active in the Man Jesus.

With this as a background, we can now say a few words about the Triune God. For the Christian Church speaks of God in this three-fold way: as "Father, Son, and Holy Spirit." And for a great many people today, this is not only a difficult but a pre-posterous way of speaking. Yet, as a simple matter of fact, it springs from the facts of experience and from men's experience of facts. It is not a matter of sheer speculation or theological complication; it is an attempt to say something about God which must be said if what has been revealed to Christians is to be maintained as true to the structure of reality.

As we have talked in these pages about God and his relation-ships with the world and with men, we have said much about him as the creator of all things, who is sovereign-ruler of all that exists, and who is also the heavenly Father. We have also said much about God's expressing himself in action, entering into and working through his world in order to reveal who he is, what he purposes, and why he has bothered with a creation at all. And we have also spoken in the last few pages of his activity in awakening and strengthening a response, an "Amen," so that the world and history and the lives of men are increas-ingly conformed to the great divine plan. Thus God has been seen as making himself understood in three ways.

In the first way, he is essentially the "ground" or explanation of all that is; the creative Reality who now and always makes his world. In the second way, he is essentially the action through which things are done, whether in creation itself or in revelation or redemption—and in this way he is supremely and decisively present and active in the Man Jesus Christ. In the third way, he is engaged in bringing about the full and complete response which creation may make to his purpose—and in this way he is supremely and decisively disclosed as the Holy Spirit about whom Christians speak. There are thus three ways, but there is one God.

Now if God is like that in his operation, he is believed by Christians to be like that in himself too. For above all else, God is true. Indeed, he is *the* Truth. He is the sure and unchanging Reality in himself who yet works outward and adapts himself to the world he is creating. So Christian faith is prepared to assert that God is not a simple unity without any differentiations or distinctions. He is one God; but he is that one God as Father and Creator, as Self-Expressive or Son, and as Self-Responsive or Spirit.

This may sound extremely intricate and involved. The ordinary Christian is not likely to concern himself very much with the delicate task of working it all out and seeing what it comes to. That is the job of the theological expert, who attempts to think through the data and arrive at some conclusion which will be adequate to the facts and as coherent and reasonable as possible.

For the ordinary Christian, the affirmation of God as Triune Deity is much more a matter of his life and his worship. The point is that the doctrine of the Trinity begins with the full Christian experience of God as Creator and Father of men, with God incarnate or "en-manned" in the human life of Jesus Christ, and with God as working in his children to bear witness, and to secure the response of service and love and obedience to, the lordship of Christ—and this is the Holy Spirit. In these, it is one God who is known, with one purpose, one will, one great concern of love. From that beginning, the Church's thinkers have proceeded to make what we might call extrapolations—reading out from the center to wider and more inclusive meanings which, when properly analyzed and understood, help to make more sense of God and his ways of working than any other theory which has been advanced.

Donald Baillie, a distinguished Scottish theologian, who died but a few years ago, once said: "I do not see how this doctrine, with its symbolical expressions, can be fully rationalized and conceptualized and worked out into a philosophical theology. But it seems to me to be an indispensable summing-up of the Christian Gospel for the life of worship . . . To those who know and accept the whole Christian story, this doctrine is the symbolical epitome of the truth about God, and its constant use in our worship helps to secure that we are drawing near to God as he really is—the God who was incarnate in Jesus Christ."

That, surely, is the big thing. And when in Christian worship, we hear such phrases as: "Let us bless the Father, and the Son, and the Holy Ghost: let us praise and exalt him for ever," or "Glory be to the Father, and to the Son, and to the Holy Ghost," we are entering into an act of adoration and praise which can disinfect us of self, lift us to heavenly places, and guarantee for us the truth and reality of God's will and way. We are recognizing and delighting in the mystery which is God. And why not? For human minds could hardly hope to fathom what it is to be God, while they can rejoice in his majesty and his glory, even as they render most hearty thanks for his loving-kindness to the sons of men.

ᴪ IO ᴪ

WHY DO WE NEED A CHURCH?

MANY of our contemporaries do not see the need for the Church. In a phrase which I have heard used, "I can go it alone; I don't need the Church."

But can any man "go it alone"? I believe the answer to that question is a flat "No." Nobody can share in that new life in Christ in isolation from his fellowmen or without dependence upon their support, encouragement, and assistance. The truth is that nobody can live *any* kind of life in isolation from his fellows. Man was made to live with others and not to live in solitary and individualistic aloofness from them.

Of course each of us has his own inner life, which is his and only his. We are each of us ourselves and nobody else. But even there, in what we sometimes like to think of as the inner sanctuary of our private existence, we do not actually live alone. We are inevitably molded by others, we react to them and their pressures upon us, we are forced to think of them and take them into account whether we want to or whether we do not want to. That is the way life is; that is the way we are.

Jean-Paul Sartre, the French novelist, playwright, and philosopher, has written a striking play *Huit Clos*, translated into English as "No Exit." The point of that play is that man is forced, willy-nilly, to be with other people. For Sartre, as his characters make clear, that is a fate which must be accepted although it is hateful. "Hell is other people." They threaten us, they make demands upon us, they insist upon relating themselves to us. Yes, they do. But many of us, who have perhaps a less jaundiced view of human relations than the French thinker, would say that while often enough other people can be our "hell," most of the time they are our "heaven." The trouble with Sartre, perhaps, is that as Gabriel Marcel (another French dramatist and philosopher) is reported to have said, he learned about human relationships "in a Paris brothel," rather than "in a family where the members cared for one another." However that may be—and it is very likely maligning a great contemporary thinker—the fact is that for most of us, most of the time, our truest human experience is had when we are most deeply and genuinely related to our fellow-men and women.

Our sorrows as well as our joys, the high and the low spots of our living, are all to a large degree occasioned by such relationships as we have with the rest of the human family and especially with those who are near to us, dear to us, hated by us, alien from our sympathies, or whatever the particular mode of relationship may be. There is indeed "no exit"; this is "*huit clos*." But that need not be the ground for our desperation, although it sometimes can be; it may just as well be the ground for our best happiness and joy.

But there is also a distance, psychologically speaking, between ourselves and others. There is the mystery of being in each human individual, and nobody else can get as close as, perhaps, he would like to get. This is true even with people whom we should like to have closest to us—the people whom we most love. Matthew Arnold once wrote of the "salt, estranging sea" which prevents the most intimate closeness from being as close as we may wish. It does not stop our being dependent; it does not alter the fact that we belong; these are natural and inevitable for each and every one of us.

We ought not to try to overcome totally that distance between human lives. We ought not to try in some brash and even blasphemous way to crash into what others think of as their secret places. This can be accomplished, this entering into the secrecy of other lives, only in the mystery of freely willed interpersonal relationships, as the current phrase has it. Even then, there is a certain "I-ness" which stands, not "over-against" the "Thou," but in distinction from that "Thou" and from his innermost personality. We are more likely to get on happily with others if we respect this special quality of theirs and do not try to intrude into what has rather inaccurately been called their "private life." Ralph Waldo Emerson once said that we should treat a friend as "a beautiful enemy." By that he meant that we should recognize and accept the distinction, the difference, above all the personal integrity of the other person.

This turns out to be the occasion for both the joy and the sorrow of human relationships—joy, in that we can in fact live intimately with others; sadness, in that we can never live as intimately as we might wish. The fact is, however, that the occasion for our sadness is also the necessary condition for our joy. It is the "otherness" of our friend which makes fellowship with him possible. If we could be identical with him we should really have nobody to be in fellowship with; you cannot have fellowship with yourself!

Now if all this is true of ordinary human experience, it is equally and even more true of our religious life and experience. Supposing that religion were just the relationship of an individual man and God—which it really is not, as we shall see—even then we should still have to carry over into it our relationships with other people, because that is the way we human beings are.

No man, John Donne said, "is an island entire unto himself." In religion, as everywhere else, no individual man can help being part of the human community, belonging to it and living in it. Yet it is also true that in religious experience, as in ordinary experience of day-by-day life, each one of us is himself and no-body else. No man can live to himself but every man must live as himself. So there is our personal selfhood, on the one hand; and on the other hand, there is our sociality, our belonging to the human race. And so, too, there is our personal relationship with God, but there is also (and just as important) our belonging to the community of men as they know God and respond to him.

No religion in the whole story of man's life on earth has ever been without its social setting. All historical religions are ex-pressed in and expressed by a community of people. And con-temporaneously, as we look across the world at the religions which people accept and believe and practice, we find the same thing to be true. Of Christianity above all this is clearly seen to be the case. It has come to us historically, as a great and living social heritage, conveyed through institutions and rites and dis-ciplines and associations in which groups have their indispensable place. Contemporaneously, it presents itself to us today as the faith of a community, with the several modes of social expres-sion to which we have so often referred. If we are concerned with Christianity as it is, we are obliged to acknowledge that it is a social religion—although the society is made up of persons each of whom is himself and can never be anybody but himself.

Many of the words we use in religious matters are derived from a Latin or Greek term which helps us to understand the basic meaning in view. Here is another place where derivation assists us. For the word "corporeal," which signifies something "bodily" in the sense of physical or material, and the word "cor-porate," which signifies a social grouping, both come to us from the Latin *corpus* which means "body." We have a corporeal body and we belong, by our very nature, to the body corporate; that is a given fact about us.

But what is a "body"? A body, surely, is some instrument or

organ or means through which, in which, by which, in terms of which, we are ourselves and we express ourselves. Our corporeal bodies are so much part of us that it is really wrong to say we "have" a body. In a most profound sense, we *are* our bodies. We are a complex kind of being, in which body and mind and soul are all integrated and knit together in such a fashion that our being, our "is-ness," is all one thing. This is why we cannot imagine a man without "embodied-ness." If we do try to imagine him, we are able to think only of a pale, emaciated, unreal "spirit" which means very little and which bears no resemblance to the warm, vital, living reality we know as a man. But man also belongs, by definition of his manhood, to the body corporate. That is, not only is his physical or corporeal structure part of him; so also is the social belonging, the sharing in life with others, part of him. Both are essential to his existence, so far as anybody can see. And if this is true in the common experience of men, it is true supremely in religious experience and in life with God in Christ. To be a Christian means to be a "member of the body of Christ." That is how the New Testament talks about it.

It is obviously true that somebody can have Christian ideas and Christian beliefs and behave in what we might describe as a Christian way, without such belonging. But then where did he get those ideas and beliefs and that standard of conduct? He got them all, he came across them, through the community of Christians down through the ages.

The Bible itself, which some foolishly assume can be set off from the corporate Christian life and witness, was written within the Christian community by people who were themselves members of it. The Old Testament was written within the Jewish community, of course, and has been taken over and used within the Christian. It has been transmitted to us, both Old and New Testaments, through the hands of the community whose book it is. The Bible cannot be read, even by the most isolated individualistic person, without his presupposing, whether consciously or unconsciously, that the Christian community was there, to have its members write the book, to have its members value what was written and so hand it down to succeeding generations, and as a living fellowship to reverence it as the Word of God communicated through the words of men who belonged to the society which enshrines the book and preserves it as a chief treasure.

When you come to think about it, the one tangible and visible result of the life of Christ in the world is this community which he created. He created it by drawing people to him and uniting them to himself in loyalty and commitment; but also in uniting them one with another because of their common loyalty and commitment to him. In the first days of Christianity, it was never for a moment thought that anybody could really call himself a Christian in the complete sense of that word unless and until he belonged to the community of Christ, the Church.

Now just so soon as I have said this, somebody is bound to rise up and begin to talk about all the dangers and evils that are to be seen in institutional religion. He will speak of the ways in which it waters down the Christian demand, or how it corrupts, by all sorts of officialism and clericalism and bureaucracy, the real Christian way of life, or through its stuffiness and dullness takes the adventure and charm out of Christian faith. All this can very well be true, in one sense; and some of us who have been fairly closely associated with the institution are probably much more conscious of, and much more disturbed about, these things than those who stand on the sidelines and criticize.

But we ought not to be surprised that this sort of thing happens. Any social expression, such as is required for a great cause, is pretty sure to show the same sort of thing. But the alternative is to deny all social expression, which means to deny all continuity and historical embodiment in Christianity, as in anything else. The alternative is to have a Christianity which is so much disembodied, un-institutionalized, that it is up in the air, in a kind of "cloud-cuckoo" land such as Aristophanes thought was inhabited by the philosophers.

If we hope to have a Christianity which makes a call upon our lives for decision, for acceptance, and for commitment, it must be located somewhere. The somewhere of Christianity is the Church, however imperfect the Church as we see it in its external expression may be. Things ought not to be as bad as they are; but one is now and again moved to feel that if those who spend their time refusing to accept and join up would take the risk of loyal membership, they might not only help to improve things but they might also recognize that it is good for our own personal humility to live with our fellows in all their imperfection and inadequacy, and even sin. At least that would be more commendable than standing by the side, carping at the Church and refusing to respect it for what it tries to be and to do.

A good illustration might be "Americanism." Some people perhaps would like Americanism to be an ethereal set of ideals which never for a moment involved them in the grim responsibilities of citizenship. In this way they could wash their hands of bad government, political corruption, failure of most of us to live up to the standards we esteem, and the like. It would be so much easier; but it would also be both silly and unhelpful. Americanism in any significant sense means that one accepts and lives with one's fellow-citizens, trying to be loyal to the ideals for which this country stands, working for better government, fighting corruption and evil in the life of the nation, and in every way doing all that one can, however inadequate or imperfect one's action may be, to bring into actuality what we regard as the purpose and aim for which the United States exists.

Something of the same thing is true of belonging to the Church.

Anyway, it is dangerous to try to have a relationship with God that is entirely private to ourselves. An English sociologist, R. H. Tawney, once remarked about the noticeable fact that the people who seek God in total isolation from their fellow men, are likely "not to find God but the devil; and his face will bear a surprising resemblance to their own." Splendid isolation leads us to be like Narcissus, who spent his time admiring his own face as it was reflected in the water. If we cut ourselves off from the community of believers in God, we shall have no criticism of our own pet notions, private fancies, and personal prejudices. That is why we are so likely, in that situation, to see God after our own image and likeness—in fact, to see him as ourselves writ large.

We need the community, the Church, to balance our personal exaggerations, to counteract our prejudices, to give us a sense of proportion, and to help establish a commonly understood—and therefore commonly understandable—picture of what Christian faith is all about.

Furthermore, we all need the help which is given to us through the worship of the Church, its rites and ceremonies, and the other activities of Christian people as they meet together and work together. Together, we can see and do far more than we can see and do alone. That is a well-known fact in human life. We always find wonderful reinforcement, strengthening, enhancing of our interest and our energy, in any matter in which we have the co-operation of a group of our friends. If the rites and ceremonies of the Christian Church are anything like what the community of Christians claims them to be, and what millions of people in their own experience have found them to be, we should be somewhat stupid to disdain to have part in them.

Certainly they can help us—and help us not only to feel good, which after all is hardly what the Christian religion is concerned with, but, much more significantly, to realize and appropriate the power which comes from God in Christ and to obtain the proportion and perspective we so much need, if we are to be complete men. These Christian rites and ceremonies may even be necessary for us, as I for one am sure they are, if we are genuinely in earnest about living the Christian life and becoming new men in Christ. They are not optional activities for odd people who happen to like them; rather, they are what the old phrase describes as "generally necessary to salvation," which is a way of saying that everybody needs them and will profit from them as he seeks that wholeness of life, salvation, which God would give to his children.

A question naturally rises at this point. That question is a very common one among men and women who have come to see that they need the Church, but who are seriously disturbed about the existence of several Christian groups of denominations. It is not the purpose of this book to speak on behalf of any particular Christian body. Our concern has been to sketch those agreed beliefs and ways which all Christians, of whatever denominational allegiance, have accepted and taught. But it is possible here and now to make some suggestions which may help an enquirer to make the choice which will be right for him.

What we can do, then, is to set down the four ancient notes or characteristics which should mark any body that calls itself a "part" of the Christian Church. It will be the reader's job to look around him and find out for himself which particular denomination seems to him to measure up to the tests and hence to have a special claim upon his allegiance.

First, a Christian denomination should hold the Christian faith in its integrity. This does not mean that it may not offer its own interpretation of that faith, nor that it may not quite properly distinguish (or permit its members to distinguish) between the big central affirmations and those secondary ones that are, so to say, peripheral to the picture.

Second, a Christian denomination should give to the Holy Scriptures, the Bible, a central and determinative place in its understanding of what Christianity is all about. It should get at its faith through reliance on the Scriptures as normative and decisive. Again, this does not mean that the Scriptures are to be taken literally, after the fashion of some extreme conservatives in our own day (the people often described as "biblical fundamentalists"), nor that reverent and careful research into their contents, dating, purpose, authorship, etc., is forbidden. It means only that the Bible does give us Christianity as a faith, in terms of its background, origins, and first development; and that in the Bible the Word of God to men is found recounted in the words which men have written down. The biblical way of looking at things, not necessarily the exact detailed accounts, is what matters most.

Third, a Christian denomination should reverently and regularly use the ancient and hallowed rites through which down the ages Christians have been initiated into the fellowship of Christ (this is Baptism) and nourished and strengthened by the life of Christ as he makes himself present and shares himself in simple elements of bread and wine (this is the Holy Communion). How these two rites are interpreted may very well differ; that they are central and are regularly and reverently used is essential—for they are, in the classic phrase, "means of grace."

Fourth and last, a Christian denomination should have a ministry which is recognized as having been authorized and commissioned to proclaim the gospel, to celebrate or administer the sacraments, and to care for and assist the people. This ministry ought to be more than a simple leadership chosen because it is convenient; it ought to be a ministry which in some genuine sense is "called" to perform the work of the Church and which receives from responsible authorities in the Church the right to act in this fashion.

These characteristics have been derived from many ancient sources, and in recent years they have been stated especially by the Anglican (or Episcopal) Churches in the general form in which I have cited them. But they are applicable to the wider Christian community; and I am interested, here and now, in their wider application. What an inquirer ought to do, I believe, is to try to look into the various Christian bodies and see how they measure up to these tests. If he then decides that one of those bodies is the one for him, he ought to make it his own. But he should never assume that people who do not happen to belong to his chosen denomination are outside the Church; and as a convinced Christian he should pray and work, so far as he can, for the eventual re-establishment in the world of a united Christian fellowship which can witness and act as one body on behalf of the one Lord Jesus Christ.

Historically Christians have often spoken about the Church in terms of its unity, its holiness, its catholicity, and its apostolicity. All these are a way of saying that Christ's fellowship is one fellowship, belonging to Christ, holding a faith big enough for everybody, and based on the very first relationship his disciples had with Christ himself. Part of the faith of a Christian, when we try to see what that has been down through the centuries, is this belief about the Church itself. So much has the Church been a part of the whole Christian position that belief in it and beliefs about it are bound up closely with Christian belief in God and in Christ and in eternal life and in the other things which make up the content of the Christian way of life. Whether one happens to like this or not, this is the way it has been, historically speaking; this is the way it still is, contemporaneously speaking.

Christianity, that is, is not a religion which we have thought up out of our own ideas; it is not something devised in our own heads. It is a faith which we accept, a life that we enter upon, a community into which we are initiated. This does not imply at all that Christianity is static and inert; on the contrary, precisely because it is something given to us, handed on to us, it is a living and growing tradition. Changes have been made and changes will be made, as we have already noted. Even so, it is not something we create for ourselves. It is something that we live our lives into. And any changes that are made, we shall discover, are made only from the inside. It is the people who are living the Christian life, committing themselves to the big matters of faith, worshiping with their brethren, doing everything in their power to make Christianity real for themselves as they share in the common experience of the community—it is those people, and not people talking on the sidelines, who effect the changes.

As a great Christian of the last century once said, "Christianity refuses to be believed first and practiced afterwards." Belief and practice go hand in hand. The only place where anybody can practice the Christian religion, in a serious sense, is inside the Church and alongside other men and women who profess and call themselves Christians.

~ II ~

WHAT IS PRAYER?

PRAYER is the Christian's "native air"; yet many, many Christians have never been properly instructed in how to pray as a Christian, and most of those who look at the Christian tradition from without have a view of prayer which to an instructed Christian seems incredibly false and crude. What, then, is prayer, in the Christian understanding of it?

It would take far too much time to discuss the many ideas of prayer which have been current at one time or another and in one religious group or another, outside the Christian tradition. Nor is this necessary, if the reader will put from his mind the preconceived ideas that he may have about prayer.

The classical statement is found in some words of an early "Father" of the Church, St. John Damascene, who wrote that "Prayer is the elevation of the mind [or soul] to God." This definition was taken over by the great medieval Christian thinker, St. Thomas Aquinas, and used by him as the basis for his discussion of the subject. The same definition, or definitions that resemble it, will be found among Christian writers on the matter in practically all ages.

Thus we see at once that for Christian thought prayer is not in its essence what so many moderns appear to think it to be: a sort of badgering of God to give us what we think we want. Prayer essentially is the lifting of our whole personalities—for nowadays we should probably not speak of our "souls" in this connection—into the presence of God. When the Old Testament tells us, representing God as speaking to men: "Be still, and know that I am God," it is saying exactly the same thing. To know God for what he is and to be in relationship with him—this is the heart of prayer as the Christian Church has taught it.

Writers on prayer have often spoken of it as "the attentive presence of God." That is an excellent phrase, even better than the definition used by St. John Damascene and St. Thomas Aquinas. For it is a basic conviction of Christian faith that God is indeed already everywhere present to his world and to men, or that the world and men are all present to God—whichever way you wish to phrase it. What is needed is that we, who are busy people engaged in doing a great many things which are necessary if we are to live here and now, need at certain times and in certain places to attend to him. He is present, but we do not realize it or act upon it, and draw from it the consequences which are implicit in it. We must pay heed, we must give our minds to it, we must divorce ourselves for the moment from our duties and labors and "know that God is with us."

The corollary of this view of prayer as the attentive presence of God, listened to and looked at, is prayer as conformity to the will or purpose of God. If we attend to God, look at him, heed him, give our minds to him, we are brought into such a relationship with him that the doing of his will becomes our aim and intention. So when Jesus prayed in the Garden of Gethsemane, "Not my will but thine be done," he was expressing what ought to be the aspiration of every Christian. God's purpose is to be effected through us, his human children, and the way in which we come to understand the purpose and conform ourselves to it, is by attending to him, by knowing him, by being in communion with him through prayer.

What we have just been saying is absolutely basic to prayer in the Christian sense. It leads us directly into an analysis of the

138

elements of prayer and the proper order or sequence in which they ought to be seen.

First there is adoration. Adoration means the praise of God for who he is and what he is. It does not ask for anything at all but simply delights in God because he is God. The West-minster Catechism has a splendid opening question: "What is the chief end of man?" with the answer, "To glorify God and enjoy him forever." To glorify God is just to adore him, both by praising him and by seeking to do his will. And to enjoy him is to delight in him, to find that relationship with him is our highest good, and to discover that in so being with him we are ourselves made into true and complete manhood. It is to be with him and to joy in that fact.

Closely associated with adoration is thanksgiving. If adoration is praising God for who he is and what he is, thanksgiving is praising him for what he has done, does do, and will do in the future. In the Book of Common Prayer this is nobly phrased: "We bless thee for our creation, preservation, and all the bless-ings of this life; but above all for . . . the redemption of the world by our Lord Jesus Christ, for the means of grace, and for the hope of glory."

God has done all this—he has made us, he keeps us in being, he pours upon us the good things which we enjoy; he has sent Jesus Christ for our completion and wholeness; he has provided us with ways to know him and be empowered by him; and he has given us the hope of eternal life with him in his presence. And he has done this and that particular thing for which we may be grateful—he has put us in this world to live with our friends, he has set the conditions in which we can realize our potentialities, he has even permitted (although certainly he has not directly willed) the untoward and painful experiences which will sharpen our perceptions, quicken our minds, develop our personalities. For all of this he is to be thanked.

Then comes an awareness of our own unworthiness, as we contrast our lives with that of Jesus and recognize that we are indeed pretty poor specimens of manhood, failing in this and that way, tarnishing our nature, distorting the image of God in us, and choosing all too often paths that will take us away from him rather than toward him.

For these deeds we are truly sorry; we are willing to confess them for what they are, and not pretend that we are completely without responsibility for the wrongs we have thought, said, and done. But there is much too that we ought to have done for God and for our fellow-men, but which by reason of our centering our thought on self or by desiring what is harmful to us and to others, we have failed to do. For that too we are truly sorry; and we do not pretend that we can disclaim responsibility here either. In fact, we make our own the words of the General Confession from the Book of Common Prayer: "We have done those things which we ought not to have done, and we have left undone those things which we ought to have done . . ." And if we examine deeply enough into the secret places of our lives, we can see what is meant by the words which follow those, in that same General Confession: "and there is no health in us." Not that we are a sorry mess of corruption and rottenness; but that in *us*, in ourselves in isolation from God, there can be no source of healthy life. For this we must depend upon him who is health, that is to say, upon God; health comes to us in our relationship with our environment, whether it be physical, social, or divine, and we need that relationship if we are to be true and complete men.

Confession of our shortcomings and failures, our sins of omission commission, carries with it for Christian faith the assurance that God forgives. Not only is an honest confession good for the soul, as the old saying has it, but a good confession enables God to take us once more into fellowship with him, to put away that which is wrong in us, and to enable us to live aright with him.

Then there is intercession for other persons and for their needs, or perhaps simply for them because we love them or because since we do not love them we want to be able to love them—and we can come to this best through bringing them consciously with ourselves into the presence of God as we attend to that presence. Intercession delivers us from too much concern with ourselves; it makes us aware of the persons and needs of others; and it unites us with them in God's all-enveloping presence, to their and to our great good. How it works we cannot know. That it works, nobody who has prayed for others can doubt.

Of course, we ought not, in intercessory prayer, to presume to tell God what he is to do for other people. That is his business; he knows it far better than we do. But we can lift others to his presence in our own thought; and that is a good thing. One consequence of this, although it is not the immediate intention of intercessory prayer, is that we shall ourselves begin to be of help to others, to care for them more, to judge them more charitably—for one cannot pray for another person without wanting to do these things.

Finally, there is prayer for what we think we ourselves may need. This is the "daily bread" for which we are bidden to pray when we follow Christ's own teaching and example and say the Lord's Prayer. It is here that a theoretical problem often rises in the minds of men and women who wonder how God can in fact answer such petitions. The best discussion of this that I know is found in the following words from an American Christian thinker of the last generation, William Porcher DuBose:

In prayer there are two ways of God, or two modes of the one way. First, he will not change nature for us, but he will, if we love him and enter into his purpose, make everything in nature, the good and the evil, good to us, work together for our good. I do not mean that he will do this merely by fitting or adjusting us to things as they are, but that he will make the things, whatever they are, actual instruments and ministers of good. . . . And second, I do not say that God will not change nature, do away with natural evils and provide natural goods, but only that he will not do it for us, in the sense of instead of us. He will not do it magically or miraculously. . . . There is absolutely no limit to what he will do through us and by us in these ways if we will be workers with him for good. God does not want to put away our sin by magic, he wants us to put it away by holiness; and so he does not work upon us by miracle, but works in us by grace; which means that he calls and moves and enables us to put away our sin by repentance and to put on holiness and life by faith. . . . What he wants is not the work but the working and the worker, the love that bears all, believes all, endures and survives all, accomplishes all, and so at last becomes and is all. And so what do we come to pray for at last, and how? By that last I mean when we have passed beyond praying for things as we think we want them and come to take them as God knows we want them. . . . I pray, then, to God only for God, to Christ only for Christ, to the Holy Ghost only for the Holy Ghost, and for everything else natural and spiritual only as through them and by them God will give me himself.

That is as beautiful and true and Christian a statement of the real significance and purpose of prayer for oneself as has ever been written. I suggest that the reader go over it again and again, ponder its meaning, and take it as the guide to his own praying when he comes to the difficulty which petitionary prayer, or prayer of asking, may seem to create.

Our last concern in this chapter has to do with the "how" of ordinary Christian personal prayer. Here a few suggestions will suffice. First, it is absolutely essential that we have stated times for prayer; if we leave it to the spur of the moment, we shall neglect it. It is also necessary that we give enough time to prayer. When a man spends only five minutes at most in daily personal prayer, he is not likely to get very far. As in so many other matters, if prayer is worth doing at all, it is worth doing as well as we can—and that demands that we give time to it, and enough time. Again, we should look upon prayer as hard work, by which I mean that we may not always find it easy to attend to God and avoid distractions and interruptions. But once more, this is something which can be attained only by trying. We can be greatly helped by reading books about prayer or by using manuals of prayer, but we should not let books become a substitute for our own personal efforts. The books will give us the line we should follow; but we must follow the line for ourselves and not spend all our time copying somebody else—however fine and experienced and devout that other person may be.

Finally, there is just a word to say about the brief prayers which can be used anywhere. Sometimes these are called "arrow prayers"—quick darts of faith, of hope, and of love, acts in which we send our thoughts to God in any place or under any circumstances. Most of the guides will have these quick prayers in various listings; but it is better if we make up our own. For myself, I like to say at odd times during the day something like this: "My God, I love thee; with my whole heart I would love thee." Or, "My God, thou art my greatest good," or, "My God, I trust in thee, for thou art my comfort, my strength, my all," or "Jesus, make me like thyself." There is a Russian pilgrim's prayer which many people have found helpful to them: "Jesus, have mercy upon me."

The point of these "arrow prayers" is that they help us throughout the day, and when away from the set place where normally we try to attend to God, to remember him, to seek to relate ourselves to him, and to grow in faith and love toward him. That, after all, is the purpose of prayer—that we shall be close to God, let him flood our lives with his strength and fill our hearts with his love, so that we may be more and more conformed to his will for us.

There is a lovely prayer which St. Richard of Chichester wrote, addressed to Jesus Christ, in which true God dwelt in true Man for the wholeness of all men. It is one that we might well make our own and say over and over again, until the truth of it is reflected in our own lives:

> Lord Jesus Christ, Savior, Friend, and Brother:
> Help me this day, and every day,
> To see thee more clearly,
> To love thee more dearly,
> To follow thee more nearly,
> For thine own sake.

⌒ 12 ⌒

WHAT IS THE MEANING OF SYMBOLS
AND SACRAMENTS?

MANY, if not most, of the important things in life cannot be spoken directly. They must be suggested, implied, hinted at. The love which we bear to our wife, the friendship which we feel for our comrade, the devotion which we have for some cause we hold dear—all of these can never be expressed in simple, plain, direct words. So we kiss our wife, we clasp the hand of our friend, we salute the flag or we raise our right hand when we swear allegiance. All of these actions are symbols: they are things done which both express and strengthen us in that state of mind which is ours.

In many other ways, too, life is experienced through symbols. There are banners which stand for our country, there are flowers which are the sign of our concern for a sick person. And there is the cross on a church tower which symbolizes the fact that in that building God in Jesus Christ is worshiped and served. That is the way life must be lived. The poet Wordsworth wrote of "thoughts that do lie too deep for tears." There are many thoughts, many loyalties, many dedications and devotions, which lie too deep for words to express.

Now man is a symbol-making and a symbol-using creature. Not only do his symbols manifest, through some outward sign, how he feels. Symbols are also a way of quickening and deepening what he feels. The kiss does not only show his love for his wife, it makes that love more real. The handclasp does more than show friendship, it actually deepens friendship. So also the sight of a banner stimulates our loyalty to our country; the flowers enhance our affection for our friend; the cross on the church tower, when we look at it now and again, increases our dedication to Christ. As we saw in an earlier chapter, man is both body and soul, and he finds that his body will express for him how his soul responds to the reality of the things for which he cares.

It is this fact about human living, as all of us know it, which is behind the symbols that are used in the worship of the Christian Church. Symbols and symbolical actions fall into three main types, and we shall say something about each of them.

First, and most obvious, are the visual symbols. The cross, the pulpit, the altar or holy table, the stained-glass in the church windows, are all of them signs which express and deepen some aspect of our Christian belonging. The cross speaks to us of Christ our Lord; the pulpit stands for the gospel in which he is proclaimed as the Lord and Master of our lives; the altar or holy table symbolizes the feeding of our weak and imperfect devotion by his gift of himself; the windows tell us of his life or of the events in the lives of his people or they present vivid and colorful representations of Christian concern for the world and its ways.

Then there are the ritual symbols—the words which are spoken. Words themselves, in fact, are always symbols, for no word is literally the thing which it indicates. A dog is not simply a "d-o-g"; he is a four-footed canine with certain specific characteristics which we have agreed to describe by the use of that particular sound. And words in a church-service are words which have a special symbolic meaning, for they are applied to, descriptions of, and ways of evoking thoughts about, the unseen reality of God and his relationship with men.

Finally, there are actions, things done. These are ceremonial symbols. We go from here to there, we lift our hands, we turn to the altar, we kneel or bow, we may even make over ourselves the sign of the cross. And here again, the same principle holds good. The action done both expresses and deepens the thought which we have, the desire we feel, the allegiance we would deepen in us. They are like the kiss or the hand-clasp; they are things done to communicate and quicken emotion or thought.

I have said that this fits in with what we know so well in ordinary human experience. It also fits in with what we know of our world. Nobody ever saw Beauty; what he has seen are beautiful things, through which Beauty expresses itself to us. Nobody has ever seen Love; he has seen only loving deeds, through which Love is made known. Purposes, values, ideals, truths, indeed everything we value most, can come to us only when we see them embodied in something which speaks to our depths and awakens in us a responsive chord.

It is not surprising, therefore, that the Christian Church should find that in its rites and ceremonies—in the words said and the things done—the reality of the unseen God is made near to his people. Nor is it surprising that in order to effect important ends, the Church employs such symbolic elements of ordinary life as bread and wine and water. This indeed is what we should expect, if a religion is to be brought home to men and women who do not live in some imagined realm of disembodied spirituality, but in the real world of sticks and stones and wood and grass. Unless it acted in the fashion in which it does act, the Christian Church would have no point of contact with people as they really are and where they really live.

There are two great sacramental acts in which Christians engage, although the major bodies whose continuity in practice of Christian sacramental rites looks back of the sixteenth century Reformation would also add five other "lesser" sacraments. The two "sacraments of the Gospel," as they have sometimes been called, are Holy Baptism and the Holy Communion.

Holy Baptism is the means of initiation into the Christian Church. It seems that it was originally associated with what would now be regarded as confirmation; in the Eastern Orthodox Church the two are still kept together. But for our purposes here, and in line with the best of recent scholarship, it will not be improper to regard Holy Baptism as initiation, and the rite of confirmation as what St. Thomas Aquinas called *augmentum gratiae* or "increase of grace."

In the sacrament of Baptism, water is used. This water is poured over the candidate, or he is immersed in living water, which means moving water, as the outward and visible sign of his being cleansed from all his sin or the consequences of sin, and enabled to become a member of the Church which is the "body of Christ." In the Anglican catechism, it is said that by the action of Baptism, the candidate is made "a member of Christ, the child of God, and an inheritor of the Kingdom of Heaven." Probably most Christians, of all denominations, would agree with this statement. It may be of interest to examine the words and see what they imply.

First of all, by Baptism the candidate becomes a "member of Christ." Before this, he has not been a member. He may be, to human appearances, good or bad; he is certainly a member of the human race, with all that this implies; but by his own human nature he is not a member of the Church of Christ. That is something which must happen to him. Thus he is the recipient of a new status; he is now what he was not before the action. In the second place, he is made "*the* child of God." I have emphasized the definite article, because it is used here alone in the three phrases of the formulation. To be made *the* "child of God" is symbolized by his being given a name, what is known as a *Christian* name—that is, a name by which he is to be known as a Christian. By nature we are all, in one sense, children of God; he is our Creator and he loves us and cares for us as he loves and cares for all his creatures, and as perhaps he loves and cares especially for his human creatures who can respond to him freely in love and service. But that, true and important as it is, cannot be put in exactly the same category as becoming, what an ancient writer called, "sons in the Son." The point of being made *the* child of God is that hereafter the baptized person, because he is a member of Christ, lives "in Christ"; he shares the life of Christ as this is made available to him through the agency of the Holy Spirit; he has implanted in him, so to speak, a new principle of life—and this new principle is nothing other than the potentiality of finding his fulfillment and completion in the Man who is both the express image of true manhood and the express Image of God-in-manhood.

Finally, he becomes "an inheritor of the Kingdom of Heaven." Here we have the assertion that by Baptism the candidate is given the assurance that he has been brought within the ambit of the Reign of God, so that he may be an obedient citizen of that Realm, fulfilling its new law of love, expressing in his behavior the will of the heavenly Father, looking forward to the "coming" in its richest and most absolute sense—whether that be in this world or in some unimagined fashion in the heavenly places. So the baptized person is possessed of a dual citizenship; he is not only a citizen of the City of Man, but he is also a citizen of the City of God. St. Augustine was the first to use these exact words; they are most apt in reference to the baptized person, for he is one to whom the assurance of citizenship in God's Commonwealth has been given and he is acknowledged as an heir or inheritor of all that City has to give to men.

This is accomplished, in Christian belief, by the use of water, which stands as a symbol for cleansing. The point here is that because we belong to a race which, as we saw in one of our earlier chapters, has accumulated a vast amount of inherited sinfulness and disobedience to the will of God, with the results which this has brought about, we are not in and of ourselves worthy of or fit for the new possibilities which faith in God through Christ makes available for us. Hence we must be cleansed. And water is an appropriate symbol for the cleansing of the personality, since it is used for the cleansing of the body of accumulated dirt.

Many people may feel that this means taking a somewhat dim view of human nature. On the contrary, I would suggest that it means taking a most exalted view. For it is a way of insisting that despite the accumulated evil in the world, every child or adult has in him the possibilities which Baptism is by way of making actual, once the candidate has been brought within the ambit of Christ's life and his empowering influence. The potentialities have hitherto been smothered and inoperative; now they are to be given the chance to develop fully and wonderfully because they are promised the enabling assistance of Christ the true Man through whom God makes himself available to his children in unmeasured fullness.

The second great "sacrament of the gospel" is the Holy Communion. Here once again symbolic means are employed. Bread is taken, wine is shared, and these elements of common human nourishment become through the blessing of God the means for the communication of the life of Christ which thus becomes the food for strengthening and refreshing those who belong to him. The origins of the Holy Communion are not only in the Last Supper which Jesus had with his disciples, on "the night before he was betrayed," they also are to be found in the custom upon which that Last Supper itself was based—the regular meals of religious fellowship which Jesus' own people, the Jews, were accustomed to observe. The relation of the Last Supper to the death of Christ on Calvary, in which he offered himself to God as a willing and obedient Servant, has also been much emphasized in the Christian celebration of the sacrament.

The Holy Communion is a double memorial, we might say; it is concerned both with the table-fellowship which Jesus had with his disciples and also with the surrender of himself to God which was consummated when he gave his life in obedience to what he took to be the Father's will. And this double emphasis is not accidental. It is found in the narratives of the Last Supper itself, for Jesus is reported to have said that the bread at that supper had that meaning, "was" his "body which is given for you," while the wine stood for the "shedding of blood" (that is, the death of Christ) through which "remission of sins" would be secured.

In other words, through the action of Jesus at the Last Supper, the Holy Communion "meal" became both a sharing in his fellowship and a participation in that which he was about to do—namely, give himself for the sake of God and God's Kingdom, that these might be made available to men.

In the Holy Communion there are several important aspects. There is first of all what we called the "memorial." Here we must be careful lest we misinterpret this word. For us a memorial can mean a looking back to something in the distant past. But for a Jew of the first century, and in the experience of the Christian as he assists at the sacrament, the memorial is not looking back so much as being with. It is not pious reverie about a past event; it is a participation in that event as it is brought into the present and made a living vital factor in the contemporary life of the believer. In similar fashion, a Jew would not think of the Passover meal as simply looking back to the deliverance at the Red Sea; he would say that it brings that deliverance into the immediate present and in doing so re-constitutes the Jewish people as what they describe as God's "chosen people." This Jewish idea is presupposed in the conception of the Holy Communion as a memorial.

Since it is in this sense a bringing of Jesus' action into the present, it includes the whole reality of his life. That reality itself includes the fact of his death. Now Christ's death was in some sense an offering made to God; we have spoken about this at some length in an earlier chapter. But the offering is effectual not alone for those who were contemporaries of Jesus; it is effectual for all men, requiring only their acceptance of Christ to make it real in their lives. As memorial, then, the Holy Communion has a sacrificial quality, for it makes Calvary present just as much as it makes every other aspect of Jesus' total life present. There is perhaps no hymnody more eloquent on this subject than the writings of John and Charles Wesley, the great English clergymen to whom both Anglicans and "the people called Methodist" look back with such justifiable pride.

Next, the Holy Communion is a participation in a present Lord. Through that action, Christians believe, Jesus makes himself present to his people. Different denominations differ as to how this takes place but they all agree that it does take place. Through the celebration, and especially in an association with the bread and wine which are used for it, the Lord is with us; and being with us, he is to be adored and "received." That brings us to still another note of the service. With the reception of the elements of the sacrament—"elements" here always means the consecrated or blessed bread and wine—the life of Jesus enters into and is united with the life of the communicant. Personalities interpenetrate; "he dwells in us and we in him." Here once more, Christian experience testifies to the universality of this way of receiving Christ. One might say that in the Holy Communion he who is proclaimed in the word of preaching is received in the heart "by faith with thanksgiving."

Thanksgiving—here is the all-inclusive aspect of the Holy Communion; and this is why, in the ancient Church, the service itself was called *Eucharist*, which is the Greek word that *means* "Thanksgiving." The whole atmosphere of the service, as well as the fashion in which all Jewish blessings were a thanking of God for that which was to be blessed, indicates that this is a right and proper way of thinking of the Holy Communion. It is not a sad or mournful act of worship; it is intended to be a great feast of joyful gratitude to God for what he has done in Christ. It is indeed Eucharist. As one of the old service forms says in an invitation the officiating minister makes to the people, "Let us make a joyful feast unto the Lord."

Finally, the words "Holy Communion," so often used to describe this service, clearly show us that the Eucharist is a fellowship, a bringing into union, of God and men, and of man with man. It establishes that fellowship, it deepens it; it sends us out to our daily work to reflect such fellowship wherever we go and whatever we do. But notice that the fellowship here is "in Christ." It is not just human chumminess; it is divine sharing with men in Christ, and hence a sharing with one another as we are enabled to "live in Christ."

When we consider all these aspects in the Holy Communion, is it any wonder that for Christian people this act of worship is the highest expression of their Christian faith and the distinctively Christian service in which they engage? How could it be otherwise? I have often thought that if the mythical "man from Mars" were to pay me a visit, and in the course of it were to ask me what Christianity really is all about, I should have one way, and one way only, of answering his question with any accuracy. I would take him to a Christian Church, where the people of Christ were engaged in the service of the Holy Communion, and I would say, "*That* is Christianity." For I would know that what he saw there and the further questions which that service would suggest to his mind as necessary to ask in order to understand what was going on, would provide the right answer and would tell him what he wanted to know.

There are also other sacramental rites in which many, perhaps most, Christians also engage.

Confirmation is essentially a prayer to God that by his Holy Spirit he will strengthen (confirm) those who have been baptized, and assist them to re-affirm (again, confirm) their promises at Baptism. It is the way in which such Christians as practice Confirmation believe that the disciple is strengthened and enabled for his life as a Christian warrior, with adult responsibilities and with adult privileges, such as admission to the Holy Communion.

Then there is Absolution. This is a rite in which, after an individual Christian has confessed, so far as he may be able to remember, his sins against God and his brethren, and has made this confession in the presence of an ordained minister of the Church, that minister, acting according to authority given to him, can "declare and pronounce" that God does in fact "pardon and absolve," deliver and free from his sins, the penitent person.

Many Christians regard marriage also as a sacrament, and all Christians regard it as having a sacramental character, even if it is not itself a sacrament. We need not speak further of it here. Then there is ordination, or the sacrament of Holy Orders. This is a rite in which the man who wishes to serve in Christ's Church as a minister of Christ to the people is "set apart" by prayer and by the laying-on of hands for his special office and work. The ordination must be performed by those who themselves have the authority to act; and in the "Catholic" Christian communions this means a bishop whose office symbolizes and expresses the continuity of the Church from the time of the Apostles, and through the Apostles from Christ himself.

Finally there is the anointing of the sick or "unction." Here, following the practice of Jesus himself and the admonition found in the Epistle of St. James in the New Testament, the priests of the great Christian bodies—notably the "Catholic" communions— place their hands upon or anoint the body of a sick or dying person, praying that through this outward and visible action God will grant health both of body and of soul.

This whole series of "lesser" sacraments, where they are employed, is once again in accord with the principle to which we referred at the beginning of this chapter. Here symbols—things said and done, physical objects or actions—are used to express and to convey invisible but real help or grace or status or office. It is the principle which is so important. That principle is signally demonstrated in Baptism and the Holy Communion, upon which all Christian people agree, however differently they may interpret the several meanings of the sacraments. Perhaps there is no greater sign of God's loving accommodation of himself to the circumstances of men, to their needs and to their condition, than by his willingness to use these ordinary and very human and natural means in order to bring them closer to himself and establish them as complete, fulfilled, and spiritually (and even, dare we say, physically?) healthy persons.

⌇ 13 ⌇

SOME PROBLEMS: MARRIAGE,
MINISTRY, MIRACLE

ANYONE who attempts to present the main themes of Christian faith and invite contemporary men and women to embrace it as the answer to the needs they feel, is likely to run up against problems which seem very serious to inquiring minds. There are many problems, but, three of them appear to be of particular importance. Oddly enough, the names of each of them begins with the same letter—the letter "m." The problems have to do with the way in which the Christian Church understands *marriage*, the question of the meaning of the Christian *ministry* and its functions in the society of believers, and the more abstract but none the less very real difficulty which many seem to find in the concept of *miracle*.

Marriage

The problem of marriage finds its center in the Christian insistence that marriage is by definition a life-long union of a man and woman, and that it is not a liaison, legalized by the government, which may be broken whenever the parties to it think that they have had "enough of one another."

There can be no doubt that this is the Christian view of marriage. In all denominations, the Christian Church is concerned above all to maintain the position that marriage is a serious enterprise in which other considerations than mutual attraction play the most important role. And in order to get at the point, it will be best first of all to make a few comments on the Christian view of sex.

That man is a sexual being cannot be in serious question. Both biologically and psychologically, the sexual drives are among the most central—some, indeed, would say that they are *the* central—drives in human personality. Nobody can avoid being a sexual creature; we have been taught this by biologists, by analysts of human motivation like Freud and others, and by our own experience. One of man's most difficult problems is thus posed to him. How can he express this sexual aspect of his nature in the best and most enriching fashion?

A great many of our contemporaries have thought that the answer to the question is the free and uninhibited sexual activity which leads men and women to engage in sexual relations how, when, and as they wish. The trouble here is that the result is bound to be chaotic in human society, and obviously enough, also to produce a kind of satiety, so that our sexuality becomes a boring and even a nauseating affair. Nobody is so jaded and stale as the person who leads a sexual life without any controls of any kind. He is a bore to himself; he is certainly a bore to everybody else.

Now the Christian way of approaching the matter is different. Human sexuality is the outward and visible sign of our desire for fulfillment, says the Christian. That fulfillment ultimately is possible only as we are in fellowship and union with God; but there are ways, in which there can be approaches to and expressions of this desire. God has put us in the world as male and female; and our intimate union with another of our kind can become, if we will have it so, a way in which we can secure fulfillment on the human level, finding in this relationship a symbol of the ultimate fulfillment which is known only when we are one with God himself.

Hence marriage has what the Church calls a "sacramental" quality; sometimes, even, Christians like Roman Catholics, Eastern Orthodox, and many Anglicans or Episcopalians, would say that marriage is itself a "sacrament."

A sacrament is an outward and visible way in which a spiritual reality is known and conveyed. So marriage can be, and in Christian thought is, an outward and visible sign of the spiritual relationship in which one human being both gives himself to and finds himself in, another of his own kind. Sex, then, is not simply an animal exercise for the relief of certain biological pressures; it is meant to be the means whereby the deepest and most genuine love of man for woman and woman for man, of one person for another person, is both expressed and enhanced.

Sex is, therefore, a sacred, not a nasty thing. It stands for and it makes manifest a relationship which is in the best sense of the word a spiritual relationship. To treat it as something other than this or less than this is to turn it into sheer animality. Of course animals are sexual, too. So is an apple! But they are sexual in a different way from man, who is conscious of his relationships and who ever seeks to make them significant and meaningful in his life. To treat sexual relations in a casual fashion and to make them intermittent and incidental to human experience is to deprive them of their best value.

A man who engages in a whole series of liaisons is very much like a dog or a cat. But man is not a dog or a cat. He is a being who can act according to plan and with due awareness of the seriousness and importance of that which he does. He can see that respect for the personality of another is crucial in human life; he can see that to use another person simply as a means to one's own satisfaction is to degrade that person into a *thing*—to deny his personality and regard him as nothing more than a convenience for ourselves.

Furthermore, the Christian regards man highly enough to believe that there is something remarkable about his capacity to make promises and having made them to keep them. He does not believe that man is an irresponsible animal, for whom no pledges can count in the long run. If man is indeed the being who makes promises, then fidelity or life-long dedication is not outside the range of possibility for him.

This is the way the Christian regards marriage. It is an undertaking in which a man and a woman give their fidelity—"pledge their troth"—one to the other. The romantic tinge, the physical passion, the desire to unite themselves so closely that physically they become one—all this is true and important; it is also good, for God made us this way. But the heart of marriage, and the clue to the Christian understanding of it, is not in the romance, the passion, and the desire for union; it is in the fidelity of one to the other. In consequence of the fidelity, the one can become so much the other that without losing identity he shares in the life of his mate to a degree that is known only to those who have thus given themselves.

This is why some Christian communions have insisted that marriage is not only life-long in intention but is impossible of dissolution. Divorce, from this point of view, is a blasphemous lie—or better, it is a denial of a unity which has been established by promise and which has been expressed in physical union as well as in the sharing of life together over a period of years.

I have spoken here very summarily indeed. The reason that I have not gone into this matter in more detail is explained not only by considerations of space, but by the more important reason that the Christian view of marriage ought to be investigated by any interested reader for himself.

At any rate, nobody should dismiss this Christian view as puritanical or as out-moded until he has tried to understand it. We have seen enough of the breakdown of marriage and the disintegration of the family in our own time, to recognize that we are confronted here with a social problem to which it is perhaps possible that the Christian understanding has something to contribute. It is precisely because Christianity takes a high view of sex, respects man's capacity to be a responsible agent, and values his promises and his ability to keep them, that it cannot rest content with the cheap and vulgar ideas that are so prevalent today. Anybody who is concerned with the preservation of human society, with the best interests of men and women, and with the enormous contribution which the family has made to our common life will want to inform himself about a way of seeing marriage that honors, esteems, and guarantees it. A view of human life which identifies it with unregulated expression of immediately felt desires and refuses to recognize the importance of order and control is a view which in the end turns man into something less than animal. Man is *man;* and his sexuality must be expressed in *human* ways.

Ministry

Every group of Christians, of whatever denominational allegiance, possesses what it calls a "ministry." The minister acts as the leader of the Christian community in worship, the exponent of the gospel which proclaims that God in Christ is present and active for our wholeness, and the shepherd of the flock of Christ to give them assistance and strengthen them in their loyalty to their Lord. This is the fact. The problem is stated in two questions: why a ministry at all? and, how does the minister differ from the ordinary Christian believer?

First of all, then, why a ministry?

161

The answer to that question is best found in the definition of the minister's task. We have said that he must act as leader of the Christian community in worship. In the orderly conduct of the Church's service, to the end that all may participate intelligently, it is necessary that there shall be responsible and trained leadership. The same is true of any other community when it meets for its public exercises. But the peculiar task of the Christian minister is to lead the people of the Church in their worship of God; he is ordained for this among other purposes and hence his ministry has always a certain "priestly" character, even if his denomination does not use the term in its description of the ministerial office.

A priest is traditionally a mediator between God and man. The Christian minister cannot himself be that mediator, for in Christian faith there is one Mediator, the Man Christ Jesus, as the New Testament puts it. But the minister can act for, represent, and carry on for the Church and within its context of life and worship, the mediatorial work which ultimately belongs to Jesus Christ alone. Thus he celebrates the sacraments and performs the other rites and ceremonies of the Christian community as the ministering agent who has been called to represent Jesus Christ. About "call" we shall have something to say a little later.

Again, the minister is one who is to proclaim the gospel by which the Church lives. This is what a sermon is concerned with. Despite a good deal of misunderstanding on the part of the laity and a misunderstanding sometimes on the part of the clergy, too, a sermon is not an address on some important moral or spiritual theme, any more than it is a topical lecture on events of the day. In the formularies of every Christian body, the minister is designated among other things as one who declares the Word of God. The "Word of God" here means what God has done, is doing, and will do in his world, as he expresses and reveals himself. So the preaching task of the Christian minister

162

is not to voice his own opinions on important themes, but to announce as clearly and winningly as he is able what God has done, is doing, and will do. This is the gospel.

Somebody must have this task. It is quite possible for a lay person to do the same thing now and again, but he is usually a busy man with other important and commendable concerns in life; he has neither the time nor the training which are requisite for such preaching as a regular task. Thus it is appropriate that within the Church there shall be designated agents, whose work is not only to lead the people in public worship but also to announce to them week-by-week the purpose of the Church and its reason for being—which is the good news of what God is "up to" in his world, as this is declared in Jesus Christ.

Finally, the minister is the "shepherd" of the flock. One of his tasks is to visit, help, instruct, strengthen, even reprove and correct, those who are seeking to share the life of God available through Jesus Christ in the Church which is Christ's body. This is the pastoral side of the ministry. Here it is often easier to understand what the minister is for. The need for counsel and advice, for encouragement and help, even for correction of wrong ideas and of unchristian kinds of behavior, is very real and present for anyone who is in earnest about his faith. Personal, day-by-day, repeated contact with the people of the Church is one of the biggest assistances the clergy render them. Here is self-giving love in a very real sense.

Some have the strange notion that it is the minister's job to "promote" Christianity. This is a mistake. The "promotion" of Christianity is the job of every person who calls himself after the name of Christ, not a special task of the ordained minister. It is, of course, true that the minister will act as leader, adviser, helper in this respect; but it is asking the wrong thing of him if he alone is expected to do the work of promotion. In any event, the word "promotion" is not a very happy one for the work which we are describing. It sounds too much like selling soap or tooth paste or automobiles. It would be better to speak of the commending of the Christian faith and its corollaries in life and in prayer and worship. To commend Christianity, not only by word spoken at the right time and in the right place and to the right person, but also by the way in which one lives with one's fellows, is what every Christian, cleric or layman, is expected to do. In that sense, every Christian is a minister, although he may not be an ordained minister.

The ancient and important view, always held firmly in the Christian tradition, is that every member of the Church shares in the continuing ministry of Jesus Christ in the world. Sometimes this truth is stated in the phrase, "the priesthood of the laity"—and here "laity" does not mean the non-ordained person but, as the Greek from which it is derived shows, the whole "people of God"—everybody who has been initiated by Baptism into membership in the "body of Christ" which is the Church. The ordained minister is as much a "layman," in that sense, as anybody else; and in that sense, too, the unordained Christian is as much a minister as the cleric.

How, then, does the minister differ from the ordinary Christian believer? The answer here is to be found in the fact that the minister is ordained. That is, he has been "called" to serve in the ministry; and when his call has been recognized by responsible authority he is set apart for the special task in the whole Christian body which is to be performed by him. The notion of "call" has sometimes been taken to mean some violent psychological upheaval or some voice speaking from the skies, telling a man that he is to do this job. Probably most of the time, and in most Christian groups, nothing of the kind happens at all. A young man grows gradually to feel that the way in which he can best serve God is along this path. He ponders this, talks it over with those who can guide him, and finally decides that he will prepare himself for the ministry. He then undergoes special training, usually in a theological school, and is ordained to his work.

In being ordained he is not made less of a man than he was before. Neither is he made more of a "man of God" than any other Christian. All Christians are, by definition, "men of God" as God has expressed himself in Jesus Christ. But the ordained minister, because he has been appointed and entrusted with this special task of leadership, proclamation, and pastoral care, has peculiar responsibilities. To him is given also peculiar privileges, such as the administration of the Church's rites and the preaching of its gospel. What he does is not done in his own name and by his own power; it is done for the Church and for the Lord of the Church. A modern saint once wrote of the minister's work: "None of it is his [the man's]; all of it is his [God's]." He speaks for, acts for, prays for, and works for the Church; and in doing that he is the appointed representative of Jesus Christ in the fellowship which Christ brought into being and through which he still brings men to God and God to men.

This is why a minister can perform his task even if he himself is inadequate to it. Any minister would gladly admit that he is inadequate—a poor human being, called to a job which is too big for him. But God uses weak vessels to fulfill his purposes, and the minister is one of the vessels God has chosen to use in the work of the Christian fellowship. So the minister's "unworthiness" does not in itself wreck his work. He celebrates the Church's rites and sacraments, preaches its gospel, and ministers in its name to the people committed to his care. He ought to be —and most ministers earnestly seek to be—as worthy of his task as is possible for him. But he is not a "plaster saint"; he is simply a man to whom has been given a job which he must do to the very best of his ability. Thus he should be respected and honored, even if some do not find him always personally a likable individual. It is not his individuality that matters most; it is the job he is ordained to do and the relationship of God's children with their Creator and Savior and Strengthener which he has been appointed to establish and nourish and deepen.

Miracle

One area where many modern men and women find difficulty is that one which might roughly be called the miraculous. It seems to such people that at this point science and religious faith are in very serious conflict. And because this seems to be so, they find it hard to accept a religion in which miracle appears to play a significant role.

Furthermore, there are certainly a considerable number of conservative-minded Christians who seem to think that they live in a world where almost anything can happen, miraculously, in answer to prayer or in some other way. They believe that the lives of the great heroes and saints of the faith have had associated with them all sorts of outlandish and contra-natural occurrences, about which stories are told which to many moderns seem highly unlikely and belief in which looks to them as a kind of hold-over from an earlier and utterly unscientific world-picture. Most people have come to believe that there is a kind of consistency, regularity, and trustworthiness in the way things run, and for them wonders such as I have described are not only highly unlikely but also very insufficiently validated through evidence which can be respected.

I do not believe that "miracles," in the sense in which we have just been talking about them, do in fact happen. The reader ought not to assume that by saying this I mean that I do not believe that the notion of the "miraculous" does stand for a very important aspect of things. I believe it does stand for something that is most important.

It is my own conviction that there is about the world precisely that regularity and orderliness about which science has said so much. I think that those who reported tales of un-natural wonders were mistaken in their reports, however right they were in their intentions. And I believe all this because I believe not only what science has taught us but also what the great religions have been trying to say for many centuries. Especially in Christianity, there is a central assurance that God works in and through everything, and that he works in an orderly and consistent fashion—in biblical language, "he is faithful." Further, he does not and will not reverse his actions and upset the plan of his world or change what we might describe as the relatively settled order of nature, to please anybody—even to please great religious heroes and saints. He works in such a way that we are able to find even in the regularities and consistencies, the constancies and orderliness, of nature and of human experience a meaning and a purpose. He makes all things work together in such a way that in the end his purposes are accomplished and the meaning which he intends emerges plainly. As St. Paul wrote in a famous passage in his letter to the Romans: "God works in every respect towards a good end, for those who love him." He does not remove the snags and snares which the established order of nature, in its more or less settled way of behaving, puts in our way. But he makes it possible for us, if we will have it so, to live with dignity and decency, and to do his will, under the conditions which he has established.

That is what "high" religion, especially the Christian faith, has come to teach about God. People who turn to religion to get them out of the regular and established order of things are fooling themselves. They are doing even worse than that. They are attempting to turn religious faith, which is the highest and noblest quality that man possesses, into a kind of cheap magic— a magic which will not work. Religion at its best is concerned with helping us to see the meaning of the given facts, not with enabling us to escape from them or twist them to our own fancy.

But on the other hand, there was a real awareness in the idea of miracle, even if the way in which this awareness expressed itself was tied up with what we now know to be incredibly bad science. This awareness was once beautifully stated in some words of the English poet of the last century, Gerard Manly Hopkins, who spoke of "the dearest freshness deep down things." Hopkins was trying to say, I think, that in our human experience there is a wonder and a glory which we do not always notice, but which is really there if we only had our eyes open and our ears unstopped. There is a loveliness and beauty, a freshness, a novelty, which can show itself to us, sometimes in what are to us most surprising ways and at moments when we are least expecting the revelation. There are unpredicted meetings, unprecedented coincidences, all sorts of newness and freshness, vivid and compelling experiences—sometimes so wonderful and so splendid that they make us hold our breath in amazement and delight, in reverence and awe.

It is that sense of the appearance, or emergence as some of our best modern philosophers would phrase it, of newness and freshness right in the midst of the regular and constant day-by-day repetition of the old and familiar things, which has given rise to the idea of miracle. The word nowadays tends to suggest to most of us very wrong and false connotations, but the fact from which the idea took its rise is a recurrent experience of people everywhere.

When the first companions of Jesus said, after one experience of theirs in his company, "We never saw it on this fashion," they were talking about something like this. Certain people do things or say things, time and again, which are so remarkable and so striking, which hit us so vividly and directly, that we exclaim in amazement. This or that happening, unexpected and unpredictable, takes place, and we, too, "never saw it on this fashion."

So the truth is that miracle, when it implies to our minds some entirely unnatural interference with what I have called the relatively settled order of things, or when it suggests a violation of the faithfulness of the divine action in the creation, simply will not do for us. The fact which is being described, however, may be very real and very important. And here we have to check the story which has been told. We may never be able to discover precisely what happened; but we can see that men in another age may very well have interpreted, in terms of their own inadequate science, what we should have described quite otherwise. Yet they may very well have had an experience of wonder and amazement connected with the person about whom they are writing which did give them a deepened faith in God, an awareness of his goodness and care, and an experience of what Hopkins described as the "dearest freshness."

Human life and experience are like that. They are not all on one dead level. There are ups and downs, high points and low points. Science is not itself concerned with these matters; it is only interested in the repetitions and the strict, or nearly strict, regularities of nature and life. But it cannot deny that these ups and downs in our experience do occur, even if it can and does seriously question them when they are described in a fashion which suggests that they occur by radically upsetting the whole scheme of things. But it is very likely that they do nothing of the sort; it is probable, I believe, that they are themselves part of that scheme and when recognized as not "contra-natural" (although they are doubtless inaccurately reported) are really the natural at its highest and most significant level.

It is also necessary for us to recognize that the great religions, especially Christianity, have been as much interested in the regularities and order of things as in the big intensive moments of

freshness and of novelty. This interest springs from a belief in a
God of order, of plan, of purpose, of faithful carrying out of
his intention for his world. But it is natural that these religions
should pay rather particular attention to the moments of intensity, of novelty, of freshness. For these are the moments when
something seems to happen to us in a very notable way. They
are the moments when we feel that we live most intensely, that
we are entering most intimately into life and its meaning for
us. Beautiful music, some haunting lines from a poem, a word
or act by a person which wakens us into a keenly felt understanding of his worth, some moment, after which everything
is changed for us—these are the times which, in Professor White-
head's word, are "important"—and by that he meant that they
set the key, give the clue, help us to appreciate what life is about,
and thus provide us with an enriched understanding for the future. So in these special moments we get a sense of the meaning
of things, we begin to grasp the purpose of life, we start to experience the real point of our human existence.

On the other hand, we can never properly make an appeal to
"miracle" in the old-fashioned sense of unnatural and scientifically absurd tales of past events. I at least do not make that appeal
because for my part I do not think things happened that way
at all. I think that the "miracle" is usually more in the way the
story is told than in the original facts about which the story
is being told. But we can see, perfectly well, how the story came
to be told in that way. We can understand that the sense of wonder, reverence, and awe which surrounded Jesus Christ, for example, almost inevitably, and at any rate quite naturally, got
itself expressed in words and ideas that were conventional
enough at the time but which we today would never think of
using. We can understand how in other experiences, the awareness of a "dearest freshness" which spoke through the event and

gave those who were on hand a feeling of new and glorious beauty and truth and goodness, almost necessarily was phrased in the way in which we read about it in the ancient documents.

We must be on our guard lest we "empty out the baby with the bath-water." Because we reject the science which is implied and cannot think that things occurred in a "non-natural" fashion, we must not reject the experience of fact, and the fact of experience, which is behind the story as it has come to us. That would be very silly for it would destroy one of the most important bits of evidence we possess as to how Jesus, if we are thinking of his life, actually made his impact on those who companied with him.

To put it more concretely, it was almost inevitable that, people being what they are and at that time having the ideas about the world that they had, the men who first repeated and later put into writing the knowledge they had of Jesus Christ, should have told about him in the way they did. His truth and goodness, his courage and conviction, his sympathy and understanding, came upon them with enormous force. The stories bear witness to this, even if they now and again have associated with them "unnatural wonder" which we nowadays are compelled to question.

Thus it is perfectly possible to raise doubts about, even to reject, the particular way in which they put it all, just as we can raise doubts about, even reject, stories in the Old Testament which are more or less of the same type. But we must also be sure to recognize that truth by which they were so impressed, we can even say overwhelmed, in the presence of the Man Jesus himself. And we can understand that they were indeed so impressed and so overwhelmed by the Man, and by their growing faith that God was with him and in him, that they used whatever words or ideas were familiar to them in the great effort to get this truth across to other people.

171

It is the truth of this impact of Jesus on men, it is the fact that in his presence and through his power they were brought to God, and above all it is their growing faith in him as the very expression of God in a true human life, which matters supremely. The words and ideas which a pre-scientific age was obliged to employ matter not at all.

♒ 14 ♒

WHAT CAN WE EXPECT FROM
CHRISTIAN FAITH?

THIS is a natural question to follow after an exposition of Christian beliefs and practices. Supposing that one is a Christian, or that one has been led to give the Christian faith a chance to prove itself in one's own experience, what will the result be? What have I a right to expect in consequence of Christian profession?

Something of the answer to this question has already been given along the way. It will be remembered that in the first and second chapters, when we were discussing the situation in which man finds himself and the needs which he feels, mention was made of proportion and perspective and power as among the greatest of those needs. What is wanted, if human life is to be complete, is the ability to see things in their right proportion, to hold them in proper perspective, and to have the power which will enable us to handle them in the right fashion. We also saw, when we were talking about sin and its meaning, that if human life is to be lived in its truest and best sense, men must have a glimpse of what that life is intended by God to be, and the strength or grace which will enable them to approximate, so far as they are able, that master pattern.

We have a right, then, to expect something like that from our acceptance of the Christian faith, our participation in Christian worship, and our effort to lead the Christian life of worship and prayer. Down through the centuries, something like this is what countless men and women have indeed found through their faithful and dedicated membership in the Church of Christ.

But a warning must be given—and here is the place to give it. Christianity is not magic, nor does it work like magic. It is a religious faith; and this fact carries with it an important consequence. One must not expect—and if one does expect one will not find—that Christianity works some instantaneous transformation. If one is looking for that, one is pretty sure to be terribly disappointed. Perhaps somewhere there are quick-working panaceas for human ills; if there are—but I doubt it—Christianity is not one of them. It has to be worked at with might and main; and it has to worked at for a long time. Only in that way are there likely to be results.

On the other hand, Christianity is not "a work." It is a relationship. The Christian gospel, we learn in the New Testament, is a gospel of grace—of God's freely given strength and help. It is not a religion of law, like much of the religion of the older Israel. Nobody can earn his salvation by what he does. It took the upheaval which we call the Reformation, to make this clear once again to a Church which had tended to forget this central truth. Whatever we do, as Christians, is done as an act of gratitude to what God has already done for us and for all men in Jesus Christ. Yet there are things which we must do. We must apply ourselves so that we can receive what God wishes us to have; and that is the labor of a lifetime, in which God's constant help and our constant striving go hand in hand, although the latter, our striving, is always a "thank-you" to God for his helping.

It is certainly true that Jesus said, "By their fruits ye shall know them." There will, then, be results from our life of Christian faith, prayer, and disciplined behavior. But the fruits come slowly, ripening over the years; they are not the quick, and therefore somewhat tasteless, growths of a single summer's day. This is exactly what we should assume would be the case if Christianity is indeed the rich and deep business that we have tried to show it to be. Furthermore, men and women are too ingrained in their self-centeredness, and their sense of alienation and frustration has gone too long unheeded, for them to be able to become different people at the wave of a hand. When Jesus said that what we all need is "repentance" (*metanoia* is the Greek word, which means "a change of mind") he was telling us that we have to become people with a different orientation from the one which we previously had. And that kind of change is not a simple business to be accomplished in a second; it is a long-range job.

This need not mean that there will be no fairly immediate consequences for the man or woman who makes an act of faith. Of course there will be such consequences. For example, there will be a sense of fellowship with others who are going in the same direction. There will be a participation in the life of a group of people who regularly do the same things together, and this will generate a spirit of sharing which can do us a world of good if previously we have been struggling along in lonely isolation. There will be the hidden and unseen, but none the less very real and effective, help which comes from sacrament and prayer. These, and things like them, will come to us; they are highly important and they are to be highly valued. But the long-range results will follow only upon the long-range commitment to Christianity.

After a life-time of Christian belonging, it was only very gradually that I came to feel the basic certainties come alive in me and acquire a sort of unshakable quality for me. Yet all the while I have had the strong sense of a backing, a security, a sharing, in the whole enterprise; and this has been true even when I was not too sure of my own progress in understanding and assimilating these certainties. The Christian Church held me up, kept me steady, gave me the assurance that I was part of a big and important fellowship.

Once again, nobody ought to think that the world's problems will be solved when and if everybody becomes a Christian. Indeed it is quite likely that many of our problems may become a great deal more serious for us and that we may find other problems which had not previously come into our ken. There is a good reason. It is only from a Christian perspective and sense of proportion that human life and man's social existence can be seen in all their wonderful possibilities and promises, while at the same time that same perspective and proportion makes clear to us failures, distortions, and depths of human degradation which had not been noticed before in the days when we were taking a less exalted view of God's purpose for man.

On the other hand, many of our problems may be handled better because we shall have the power for right dealing. What we need, in so many of our most serious difficulties, is the will and the strength to take a stand for justice, to speak up for mutual forbearance, to work insistently yet patiently for improving such matters as racial, national, international, social, and economic failures and tensions.

The new sense of the seriousness of our problems, coupled with the power to work at them bravely, is, for the Christian, associated with what the theologians have called "justification by faith." This phrase may puzzle some people, while others will think it to be only a piece of meaningless religious jargon. But it is neither puzzling nor meaningless. It is simply factual.

What is involved in "justification by faith" is simply that when a man has done the best he can do in any given situation, he can still do one thing more—he can leave the ultimate results in the hands of God. If a man has truly done the best that he can do, and has done it in good faith and with utter integrity of purpose, he can honestly commit whatever he has done to God, and then not worry too much about the final conclusion of the matter. Only in this way can anybody find true peace of mind. After all, we know quite well that everything does not depend on us. We are well aware of the imperfection of any action in which we engage. Why not recognize this frankly, humbly, and gladly? The Christian can have the confidence that God, in his infinite wisdom and all-pervading governance of the world, will use what we have done for the best ends possible under the circumstances and for the accomplishment of his purposes in those circumstances.

In our own religious struggles—above all perhaps, there—the same is true. We must rest back finally on a trust in God and in God's doing for us "better things than we can desire or pray for," as the old collect in the Book of Common Prayer puts it. If we let God have our lives, in as great a measure of self-commitment as we can possibly manage at any given time, we can be sure that he will "take care of us."

His taking-care will not necessarily mean that everything will become nice and easy. If Jesus Christ himself had to go through the apparent denial of all his mission was about, if he had to experience the sense of failure in its accomplishment, if he died on the Cross, we ought not to think that our own lives will be a bed of roses. Life is never that way, as we all know. The question is whether we shall have the strength to take what comes, rather than the wish always to hunt for some easy escape. Thus we read in the New Testament that "God works in all respects towards a good end for those who love him." This does not imply that we shall have a soft and easy life. It assures us that no matter what happens, God will never let us go, provided only that we let him take our hand.

The Christian can expect to learn how to live bravely and joyfully even when things are not going pleasantly. Perhaps each of us has known at least one person who illustrated this attitude. I can think of one such—an old lady, almost completely blind and deaf, living in a home for elderly people, with no money of her own and with none coming to her from anybody else. But her joy in life and the serenity with which she now meets, as she has always met, the almost overwhelming difficulties she has to face, make her a brightening person to be with. Her religious faith, to my mind, is pretty much out-of-date; she certainly does not take a modern position on most of the matters with which we have been concerned in this book. But the significant thing about her is that she has the basic faith which gives her the ability to "take life" bravely, indeed happily. That is why she is such a radiant person, giving joy to all those who are around her. She has Christian faith, however outmoded its details may be. And that same faith could be shorn of its outworn theology and its antiquated way of regarding the Bible, without for a moment losing its strength and its force in her life.

What, then, can one expect if one becomes a Christian? One can expect some immediate consequences—fellowship and acceptance from a Christian congregation, help from the Church's worship, sacraments, and common life, entrance into a relationship with God through one's personal prayer. One can expect to begin the acquisition of a new proportion about things, a new perspective on them, and hence a truer grasp of the way things really do "stack up" in this world of ours, at a deeper level than surface appearances might indicate. One can expect slow growth in grace or power for the meeting of obstacles, the changing of character, and the work of bringing decency and justice into the world. One can expect a gradual development of the assurance that one is on the right way and that one is surrounded by a great cloud of witnesses who have gone that way in past ages. One can expect some sense of cleansing from sin, some sense of the loving care of God, some sense that one is going in the direction of fulfillment and the completing of one's human nature. And one can expect hard work.

Nothing important comes easy. The Victorian scientist Thomas Henry Huxley said that while "it does not take much of a man to be a Christian, it does take all there is of him." Doubtless he meant that in a somewhat derogatory fashion. But what he said is true all the same. Anybody can be a Christian, whether he is "much of a man" or not. Christianity is for everybody, not for some select few. But if a man lets himself in for Christianity, it is going to take "all there is of him." It will demand whole-hearted loyalty and devoted effort, in a great many ways which perhaps at the start one has never even contemplated. Yet there is one result which will compensate him, if it may be put in that way, for all the trouble it may cause him.

That result is the slow but certain growth within him of a conviction that life has meaning, that man is meant to live with decency and dignity, and that neither our fears nor our anxieties can destroy the ultimate confidence which comes from faith. In words from the New Testament, "we know whom we have believed, and we are persuaded that he is able to keep that which we commit unto him."

To be a "new man in Christ Jesus" is worth anything and everything that we may have to do or be called upon to undergo. For that new man is the *real* man; he is the man who is being conformed, slowly and painfully perhaps, to Christ who is the express Image of God in manhood, the complete and fulfilled manhood which is God's will and God's purpose for us all.

And now we can go on to speak of possible attitudes to life and the way in which Christianity makes possible that one of them which is the most satisfying because it is the truest and best. The way to get at this is by seeing how people, as a matter of common observation, look at others and at the world.

Some look at life "as their oyster," as the old saying has it.

Their one thought is exploitation, to get what they can out of things, out of others, out of life itself. Others look at life as spectators; they observe and watch, perhaps they describe and discuss; their dominant thought is exploration. But there are some people—and these would appear to be the happy mortals who have learned one of the secrets of living—who regard life and experience with what Baron von Hügel, the great German-Scottish thinker of the early years of this century, once called "eager expectancy." They look for and wait upon the coming of new and great things; they keep their whole being open for fresh light and for more truth; their attitude to life is one of expectation.

The three words that I have chosen to use to describe these attitudes are not entirely adequate, but perhaps they will serve a purpose. At any rate, the attitudes themselves are pretty obvious—we all know them, in ourselves and in others. And in each of us some of each of them will be found, and rightly. The important question is, which one predominates and controls? For upon the answer to that question will depend the fullness of life for every man.

To some degree it is necessary that each of us should have the exploiter's attitude. There is much in the world which is here, evidently, for our use. We cannot run away from our dependence upon things, and this means that often we must use them for ends which seem good to us. We ought not to "use" other people, certainly; yet even here there is a sense in which we must all make use of their talents, abilities, interests, and the like. Contrariwise, if we exploit natural resources to such an extent and in such a way that we destroy the very basis of our subsistence, we have been silly and even sinful, for we are not the lords of the universe and we are not called upon to despoil the world for those who come after. Similarly, when we make use of other people, we are not to do so in such a fashion that they are merely objects of our amusement and pleasure, with total disregard of their personality and their essential humanity. They are not our playthings. If we depend upon their helpfulness, we do not have to make them means to our own ends, with the result that they are cheapened or hurt. If we do this, we are much more than silly; we are guilty of our brother's fall from manhood into mere object-hood.

Quite rightly we must explore. This is an attitude to life which everybody must share to some extent. The scientist provides one very good illustration of the right kind of exploration; the natural historian or the lover of nature is another. Each of us wants to know about things, to discover truth, to work things out with explanations which follow on examination and exploration. It is natural and good to do this. If the religious man may be described as the person who says to the unmeasured realities of the universe, "Humbly I adore thee, Deity unseen," the scientific man and the inquiring man rightly says, "Humbly I explore thee, Verity unseen."

But where that humility is absent, exploration goes wrong. The man or woman who is content simply to explore, but without respect for that which he is exploring, is a scientific blackguard, a rogue, or a "peeping Tom."

Above all is this true when it comes to human relations. There is nothing so dreadful as the person who regards other people with curiosity unmixed with reverence. The man who looks at us knowingly and attempts to violate the secret places of our heart is a man who is not only hard to get along with but a man who lacks some of the qualities which make for genuine human respect and dignity. It is right and proper, then, that we should explore the world of nature, the realm of history, human society, and the experience of men. But it must be done with reverence;

and as our knowledge increases, so "more of reverence in us grows"; for no man can be a spectator of life and still be a true man, and no man can be an explorer of life without reverence and remain human in the truest sense of that word.

But the attitude of expectation is best of all. And it is also the peculiarly and specially Christian attitude.

To look at life as a rich, dynamic business, pulsating with the energy which God has put there, is to find it always fresh, interesting, enriching. To expect more than meets the eye, to let our experience be dominated by the hopeful conviction that "God hath yet more light and truth" which he will break forth in this or that place, redeems our day-by-day existence from staleness, sterility, and fatigue of mind and heart. It can make a tremendous difference for a man to see that there are heights and depths, in nature and in human history, and in the lives of men, from which there can come, and will come, surprises that give variety and freshness to existence. Daily experience is illuminated when we expect that out of the apparent monotony of "the trivial round and common task," there may emerge some many-splendored thing.

So far as I can see, there is only one way in which this expectant outlook can be maintained. That is by faith in the living God, who is working out his purpose in his world, whose indwelling life moves through the creation, and whose indefatigable will is controlling the destiny of men and nations. If God be there, we can look at life with "eager expectancy." But if God is not there, it is plain that such an attitude is stupid and absurd. If the world has no meaning, no purpose, no sense; if it is getting nowhere, then it would seem wiser simply to try to exploit it and explore it, all for our own sakes. The only reason that can be advanced against this attitude is that in the end we shall bring ourselves and our fellow-men to ruin; but what does that matter if all goes down to utter darkness and senselessness?

On the other hand, if God is in it, pouring his energy into it, bringing new things to pass within it, using it to realize mighty ends, then there is romance and mystery, adventure and gaiety —and there is also high purpose and dignity. Human existence is made a strangely attractive thing, other people have a wonder about them, and the world of nature is fresh and lovely. Perhaps this is why the saints are such bold and happy people. For this is the way they have looked at life. Think of St. Francis of Assisi.

It is Jesus Christ who gives us the supreme illustration of expectation and expectancy. If ever there lived One who expected great things of God, whose attitude towards his brethren was likewise expectant of goodness and splendor, it was he. He expected, and by his acting upon that expectation brought about, a response to him which could make men noble and true in their relationship with their Maker. What he did to Simon Peter was repeated in what, when risen from the dead, he did to Saul of Tarsus. And what he did to those two men is repeated day after day in those who have let him teach them something of the wonder and mystery of life, so that they look at it with reverence and approach it with joy, expecting that God will do great things in it and in them.

This truth can be perverted into a silly unrealistic kind of false optimism. But it need not be. And in any event the optimism which springs from a robust attitude of expectation, from "eager expectancy," is a more enriching and ennobling attitude than the kind of pessimism which looks at everything as dull, dead, senseless, inane. Christians are people who can be optimistic; their optimism springs not from any confidence in themselves, but from their conviction that this is God's world, that he is a God of goodness and justice and truth, and that the world can never get itself out of his all-sovereign hands.

So the Christian can look for results. And one of those results is precisely this capacity for expectancy as his dominant attitude. It cannot be worked-up out of our own experience, for that is likely to leave us cynical much of the time. Christian expectancy comes to those who company with Christ in his fellowship the Church, and in whole-hearted dedication to the will of God for his world.

☙ 15 ☙

SHOULD I TRY IT?

THIS is the big question for the reader if he is an inquirer into the possibility of Christianity as a vital faith for a modern man. Suppose that what we have been arguing is true or that, at the very least, there is a good deal to be said for it. Is it, then, worth trying?

To that question I should wish at once to return, by way of answer, another question: Why not?

People give many different reasons why they think they should not try Christianity. They say that church services will bore them. That may be perfectly true. But much of the trouble comes at this point because people persist in thinking of church services in the wrong way. When they have got beyond the rather silly idea that it should amuse or entertain them, they seem to assume that a church service should give them a thrill or produce an overwhelming experience. Then they go to church and find that they get no thrill and do not have an overwhelming experience. As a matter of fact, the purpose of worship in the Christian Church is not at all to give us a thrill; it is to give us a chance to make our own commitment to One who is greater than ourselves—to praise and glorify God, and by indirection to enrich our experience of the life with God.

Some say that they do not care for sermons and that such sermons as they have heard have been less than completely inspiring and not often very informing. Very well; that also may be true. But the point of attending church is not to hear sermons, although often enough, if we do listen to them patiently, we shall hear the gospel through the words of the preacher. And anyway, to be with our Christian brethren is in itself a good thing, witnessing to our sense of need for help and our readiness to participate with our fellows in their similar case.

More often, though, it is not superficial matters like this which get in the way. It may be that an inquirer does not know whether he is quite ready at the moment to accept the whole Christian faith. He feels that there is a great deal in it, but he still has some hesitations and doubts. Probably everyone feels that way some of the time, whether he is a practicing churchman or not. But how on earth are we to come to understand what Christianity is all about, how are we to be brought to the point where we can endure our hesitations and doubts and yet make a commitment to the big things in Christian faith, unless we get inside it and see what is going on?

There is not much to be said for the man who is always criticizing the players but never himself trying to "get into the game." What right has he to be a carping critic or a hesitant observer, unless he knows something of the game which is being played? If one wants to know what Christianity is all about, if one wants to grow in understanding it, there is only one place for that—it is inside, with the people who are themselves working at it.

Nor is this a wrong thing for a liberal-minded man to do. If a man has a mind that is really open—not at both ends, so to say, with the result that nothing stays with him for long, but with a generous desire to see what others are doing and if possible to learn from them—he will recognize that it is right for him to try Christianity, with all his heart and soul and mind, to see if it will prove itself true for him. He assents to the big things about it—the sort of things we have been describing in this book;

the smaller things, the secondary matters, the peripheral questions, will take care of themselves sooner or later, either by his seeing that they are in fact small, secondary, and peripheral, and hence not worth bothering about, or by his coming to understand how they fit into the total pattern and can therefore be accepted as part of it all.

Or again, somebody may feel that the Christian religion will begin to make impossibly difficult demands upon us, once we give it a try; and that is not an idea that appeals to us very much. But is it not true that anything in life that is worthwhile makes such demands upon us? If we honestly think it is worthwhile, we are prepared to accept the rules and try to meet the demands. They may be impossible, but at least that is better than if they were so easy that they did not exert any pressure upon us whatsoever. A religion like that would have no effect at all.

Christianity may be—and as a matter of fact it is—something that will take all there is of any man who accepts it seriously. It expects of him that he will really work at it. And it does not guarantee that things will happen in a flash; it supposes that it will take time, as well as effort, for a man or woman to begin to appropriate what it has to offer. Christianity is a very big business; it is concerned with the most important issues any man can ever face. It is either the greatest fraud that was ever proposed or it is the greatest truth about the world and the God who made it and the men who live in it, that has ever appeared in human history. Something like that will inevitably be difficult, will certainly make demands that may seem impossible, will surely require whole-hearted effort. I do not see how it could be otherwise.

For my part, I am convinced that the inquirer ought to give Christianity a try. If he knows something about the sense of "quiet desperation" and the disquietude which troubles the hearts of men; if he is really looking for a faith which will give him proportion and perspective and power; if he wants to be made a complete and full man—he can ill afford to pass by the Christian claims. If he wants to find a faith that is concerned with truth, that will treat him as a free man, and that will develop in him the spirit of charity—he can ill afford to neglect what the Christian Church has to say.

Suppose, then, that the inquirer decides he ought to give this Christian business a real try? What should he then do? First, he should continue looking closely into what the Christian tradition has said. It is not likely that he can do that all by himself. As we have seen, it is not in the nature of the Christian religion to be a solitary affair. This is something that we do together, if we do it at all. So one line of action is to get in touch with the nearest local minister. Perhaps the reader has never met him; or perhaps, if he has met him, he may not have felt free to talk with him about things like this. But why not attempt it? Why not talk this business over with him? Why not give him a chance to help? That is what he is there for.

Second, the inquirer should go to church some Sunday and see what it is like. And he should continue going until he becomes familiar with the service and is able to participate in it, so far as conscience will permit; that is the only way he can share the experience of those to whom worship is an enriching and ennobling part of their life. Nobody will be mortally wounded by attending a few church services. And even if the service is not thrilling, the sermon not exciting—who knows, though, for it may just possibly hit the inquirer between the eyes or speak exactly to his condition—at any rate, he will have got inside and he will have begun to see what Christian worship is all about.

Third, how about some attention to the business of Christian prayer? Prayer is an indispensable part of human life, if that life is to relate itself to the whole of man's environment and grow into completeness. Has the inquirer really tried to pray in any fashion beyond the childish request for what he wants when all other ways of getting it have failed? Has he sought to know the presence of God? Has he disinfected his life of too much self by turning himself toward the God who can make our pettiness grow towards his greatness?

The whole business is now up to the reader. Somebody once wrote these fine words: "Christianity is an experiment which ends in an experience." Perhaps that will be true in the reader's case. In any event, why not give it a chance to prove itself true? There is only one way to give it the chance, and that is to give it a try.

BIBLIOGRAPHY

THIS list contains a few books which the reader may wish to consult in pursuing his study of Christianity; it does not pretend to be complete or exhaustive.

Bethune-Baker, James F. *The Faith of the Apostles' Creed.* Greenwich, Conn.: Seabury Press, 1955.

Burnaby, John. *The Belief of Christendom.* London: S.P.C.K., 1958.

Caird, G. B. *The Truth of the Gospel.* New York: Oxford University Press, 1950.

Ferris, T. P. *When I Became a Man.* New York: Oxford University Press, 1957.

Hessert, Paul. *An Introduction to Christianity.* New York: Prentice-Hall, 1959.

Neill, Stephen. *Christian Faith Today.* New York: Penguin Books, 1955.

Richardson, Alan. *The Gospel and Modern Thought.* New York: Oxford University Press, 1950.

Spurrier, William A. *Guide to the Christian Faith.* New York: Charles Scribner's Sons, 1952.

Two useful books, which study the life of Jesus Christ and help the reader understand who he was, what he did, and why men have believed him to be the manifestation of God in human life, are:

191

Bethune-Baker, James F. *Early Traditions about Jesus*. Greenwich, Conn.: Seabury Press, 1956.

Knox, John. *Jesus: Lord and Christ*. New York: Harper & Brothers, 1958.